Brexit
How the Nobodies Beat the Somebodies
By Sebastian J Handley
ISBN: 978-1-9997156-9-4

Published by

i2i Publishing. Manchester.
www.i2ipublishing.co.uk

For Dave

My name is Sebastian and I am a nobody, and this is the story of how I got together with some other nobodies, overturned the government and changed the course of European history.

I should have written it all down as I went along and if I had known how momentous it would eventually become, then I definitely would have, but while it's still fairly fresh in my mind I will try to piece it all together using my Facebook, email and phone history to record exactly how The Revolution unfolded.

Throughout my life, from watching The Young Ones, to student marches, to discussions in the salon, there have often been tongue-in-cheek references to 'The Revolution' mostly making the assumption that it was some type of historical end-of-the-rainbow that would never actually happen; and if anyone had challenged me to put money on it, I would have bet the farm that it wouldn't. But it did, and when it happened it was nothing like any of our predictions – there were no burning barricades, no petrol bombs, no big marches, no occupations and no guillotines – it was a very British revolution.

Such events are fantastically rare and I was very fortunate to have a ringside seat, not at party headquarters or in the press room, but on the campaign trail where it was really won and lost. So, for all you young activists out there fulminating about the injustices of the world, I'm going to go through all the events leading up to the changing of the guard, listing everything that we did right and wrong and everything our opponents got right and wrong so you can do it too.

Initially it was my intention to call this book *'David Cameron – My Part in His Downfall'* but I

5

decided against it owing to the fact that my personal dealings with Mr. Cameron are rather limited: In 2013, I set up a community book exchange in a phone box in Lewisham. The story of the *Lewisham Micro Library* is for another day, but having set it up, I handed it over to some new 'librarians' and moved to Brighton with my (pregnant) wife Vicky to raise a family. I was bemused to then be contacted by the Prime Minister's office in 2015 informing me that I had won a 'Point of Light Award'. Dave sent me a very nice tweet and I responded politely offering him his very own guided tour the next time he visited Lewisham.

UK Prime Minister
@Number10gov

Following

Sebastian Handley is today's #PointsofLight for converting a disused telephone box into London's smallest library #LewishamMicroLibrary

RETWEETS
28

FAVORITES
34

7:31 PM - 5 Mar 2015

10   1

Elaine Willis @elainey60   5 Mar 2015

@Number10gov well your closing all the others

↩   🔁 1   ♥ 2

Additionally, I received an excellent certificate resplendent with his signature (which I must get framed and hang up when I get the time) and as if that wasn't enough he even took time out from his EU negotiations to send the Handley family a Christmas card that year! Thankfully my wife was at hand to photograph the ecstatic moment I opened it. I posted this on Facebook and everyone was extremely jealous.

John Lyons: *Jesus, nobody wants a card from a nasty right wing old twat, so don't send him one back eh?*

Sebastian Handley: *Now I see how wrong I was ... Vote Tory everybody!*

So, what to do? Dave had been nice to me, sent me a friendly tweet, and a Christmas card! Could I really spurn his gesture of goodwill? Could I really, magnanimously engage with him one day and oppose him with every sinew of my being the next? Well yes, I could, because from the moment it became clear there would be a referendum I saw it for what it was: a once in a lifetime battle, which we had to win and which he had to lose. If he was my brother, my son, or my best friend it would have made no difference. We *had* to win.

But why did we have to win? Why did I care? Well in most aspects of my thinking I take a Burke-ian view that society is best reformed by millions of people making billions of considered incremental adjustments; this should have lead me to conclude that we should stick with the EU in the hope of reforming it. So why here did I take the Paine-ian view that there had to be a clean break? Because the EU was deliberately designed to be un-reformable, so it had gone from being merely dysfunctional, to being an outright liability, from an incubator of tyranny to a generator of it. Yet far from being apologetic or circumspect about what it had become it manically drove onward. Every crisis was seized upon as justification for moving decision making ever further from the control of voters, and as democratic accountability diminished, dysfunctional government expanded, fuelling the next crisis, the *'solution'* to which was always to be *'more European'* (less democratic). They were hypnotised, caught in an endless feedback loop of decline that they couldn't escape from. They weren't interested in listening or changing and they were only interested in negotiating as a means of prevarication. They had to go, or rather, we did.

Ok so who was the father of the revolution? Farage? Johnson? Gove? No. Cameron. By incrementally eating away at the Tory Party's core support Farage had brilliantly manoeuvred Cameron into a position where he had to offer a referendum. Blair, Clegg and Cameron had all promised referenda when in opposition which they reneged on when safely in government but with UKIP becoming the third most popular party in Britain, and the prospect of a hung parliament in 2015 Cameron had no choice but to defuse UKIP's appeal by offering his own referendum, and his Bloomberg speech is the obvious beginning of our story.

Wednesday 23rd January 2013
If you are not familiar with Cameron's Bloomberg speech you are not missing much, the Vogon poetry of oratory, it's so monumentally boring its actually painful to read. Clearly intended as a definitive vision of the future, the best that can be said of it is that it illustrates perfectly the odyssey of bullshit we managed to extricate ourselves from by leaving. But crucially buried amongst all the oxymoronic caveats was the promise of a simple in/out vote. Why did he make the political error of proposing a clear binary choice? If he had half the guile of Blair or Wilson he would have offered a referendum he could have wormed out of if it didn't go his way, but he was so overconfident in his political abilities he proposed a black and white choice. This was his first mistake.

Perhaps he genuinely wanted to settle the issue once and for all, or maybe he felt the starkness of the decision would make people quail with fear at the prospect of leaving. I don't know, you would have to ask him, but certainly, trying to frighten the British into acceptance was a feature of his subsequent campaign.

Am I being unfair to Farage? Probably a bit, but let's imagine that Farage and not Cameron had the power to decide wording of the referendum. I doubt Farage would have worded it in such stark language that losing would have meant oblivion for the losing side. I suspect he would have preferred a series of referenda, one on the sovereignty of British law, one on payments to the EU and its proxies and one on trade that would have unpicked our membership vote by vote. But I admit I'm hypothesising.

I have long thought that Cameron was over-rated as a political strategist. Sure he was a winner, but who had he beaten? He had beaten Clarke for the leadership, then he had beaten Brown during the Credit Crunch and he would go on to beat Miliband but hitherto he had been lucky in his opponents; lucky that is until he came up against us. And that is why over anyone else I would hail Cameron as the unintentional father of the revolution: with an excess of confidence and lack of guile he designed the arena. God bless you Dave, your misjudgement has saved our country. I love you! ... and thanks for the Christmas Card.

Thursday 7th May 2015
General election. Conservative Majority. Game on.

Tuesday 14th July 2015

Writing in the Guardian, Owen Jones who hadn't much interested me up to that point wrote an essay that was a bolt from the blue – *"The left must put Britain's EU withdrawal on the agenda"* He was hedging his bets but still it was the most electrifying piece I had read since Andrew Sullivan stopped blogging.

August 2015

Immediately after the election the Referendum Bill began its passage through parliament. Why do you think Cameron introduced the bill right at the beginning of the term? You may have your theory but mine is that he knew the EU wasn't going to get any easier to sell: the Eurozone crisis wasn't about to get any better, the Islamic war wasn't about to get any smaller, and there were plans afoot for a *'Common Defence Policy'*. As independent European nations like Norway, Switzerland, Iceland, Georgia and Greenland surged ahead and Eurozone nations fell deeper into civil war and economic decline, Cameron made the sensible choice of going to the country in the afterglow of victory, before the mid-term blues set in. Just seven months after the election the Referendum Bill received Royal assent.

A brief aside about referenda. If I am so right that EU membership was so wrong then why were we the underdogs? Why weren't we streets ahead in the polls?

Throughout modern history and across the world referenda have tended to confirm the status quo. Voters are instinctively cautious and tend to prefer the devil they know, so it is highly unusual for people to endorse a big change in a referendum. This is why in 1973 Heath took Britain into the EEC *without* a referendum. One was then held in 1975 which asked whether Britain should *remain* in the Common Market which the electorate endorsed. So it is impossible to have a neutral choice in these matters. There will always be an existing condition that will enjoy the advantage of incumbency, whose advocates will be able to loftily dismiss the alternative as unrealistic and unworkable. So for the existing condition to be rejected in a referendum it's failure has to be totally apparent, and the alternative obviously safer. This is why defending the status quo was a huge advantage to Remain and their staunchest supporters would concede that if Britain had suspended its EU membership and held a vote as to whether we should re-join, they would have lost by a landslide.

I began pulling together my various anti-EU rants into one master essay. My vision for it was that it would be a pamphlet that would comprehensively answer any and every pro-EU argument. The problem however is that the EU is geographically large, politically complex and has existed for several decades, so any such essay would have to be fairly broad. It quickly became obvious that I was writing a book rather than a pamphlet, and with my tendency to turn everything into a grand project I started getting anxiety attacks. *'Why Britain Should Be Independent'* was becoming an unfinishable magnum-opus, and even if I could finish it, it would be too long to read and finished too late to make any difference.

I think one good strategy for life is to surround yourself with people you respect and then listen to them. One such person in my circle is Joe Hoover, then a lecturer on Human Rights and International Relations at Queen Mary College.

Nervously I posted him my umpteenth draft, and then re-read it cringing with embarrassment at what he might make of it. His critique was bruising but it was what I needed. Every unsubstantiated opinion and exaggerated claim was put down without fuss. I had clustered my most impassioned rhetoric at the end as I thought it might switch people off to start ranting early on, but that anyone who had soldiered through the first 3000 words would probably be prepared for the fire and brimstone conclusion. Joe tactfully said he didn't have time to read the whole thing but that his main criticism was that my essay was far too long.

I asked Joe how he thought I should write.

He said I should try to write essays as if I were writing a song:

1, Simple sequence of arguments.
2, Say one thing in each sentence.
3, Don't say anything twice.

I incorporated all his corrections – except I ended up making it about 2,000 words longer!

14th September 2015
On this day after months of revisions I finally published *'Why Britain Should Be Independent'* on my WordPress site, but I didn't send it to the world. Instead I used its presence in the public domain to shock me into reading it as if for the first time.

Here is probably a good time to point out that although I live in Brighton, I work as an architectural technician in Farringdon. This meant I spent three hours travelling to and from work every day, and this was when I read and wrote furiously using my smart phone and my mini iPad. Most days I would sit opposite Tony, a wonderful tailor from Northern Ireland who worked at the National Theatre, and we would talk about art for a bit before he would start watching a film and I would start tapping away. Sometimes he would ask what I was writing, and I would talk vaguely about terrible songs that no one would ever listen to. But although the struggle ended up consuming my life, for a long time the commute allowed me to keep my campaigning separate from everything else.

This is probably also as good a point as any to explain why I positioned my campaigning emphatically on the left. Obviously, it's impossible to campaign everywhere all the time, because then you will become paralysed by the enormity of the task. You have to pick your fights, so I decided to concentrate my campaigning where it would be most effective, so I never bothered to post anything on the Telegraph discussion pages, only the Guardian's. After all, if someone reading the Telegraph was unpersuaded then it was unlikely that I would be able to change their mind. But I felt there was progress to be made posting on the Guardian's forum for several reasons:

1, The Guardian was overwhelmingly pro-EU and in a campaign, you want to be engaging with people who are not on your side. Every minute spent agreeing with someone is a minute wasted. That's the classic mistake of the Labour Party – they talk to themselves.

2, The polls were about 50/50 so just a 1% swing would win it, this meant abstentions were important and the left were simply more persuadable than the right. Take for example Paul Mason. Here we have a highly intelligent man who has written a study of struggles against neoliberalism called, *'Why its Kicking Off Everywhere'*. If I were to ask Mason whether he believed that there should be democratic oversight of the powerful I have no doubt that he would answer in the affirmative. But did he believe in independence? Er ... yes ... But not yet! ... So we see even among the intelligent progressive left a circumspection, a genuine uneasiness that all might not be rosy in their precious EU garden.

Granted there may have been some Telegraph readers who were in the Heseltine/Ken Clarke camp, but they were comparatively small in number and generally not worth arguing with. There were simply more votes (and abstentions) to be won by engaging with the left than the right.

3, This was a war of ideas, and ideas are circulated on the Internet. Left-wing people are public with their politics, whilst right-wing people are private about their politics. So, there was more chance of a left-wing argument for Brexit going viral than a right-wing one.

4, And finally, because in my heart I believed it was true. The argument for independence really *was* a progressive argument for ordinary people to be able to vote for better laws and leaders. The only reason why Guardian readers tended to disagree was because they conflated the EU with a progressivism that it didn't deserve, and Brexit with a right-wing agenda that we didn't deserve either.

So straight away we find we have a problem with terminology that is going to crop up all the way through this story: We all use words like *'left' 'right'* and *'progressive'* as pejorative terms of convenience and assume that everyone understands the same thing by them. But the whole point is that the reality and the terminology had become inverted. *'Left'* and *'right'* were now just badges people stuck on things to indicate what to love and what to hate. Indeed, it got so ridiculous that by the end the *'left'* were campaigning against representative democracy and the *'right'* were campaigning against neoliberalism!

Confused? Well no one could blame you because the whole point was to confuse. As we go through the story we will see that a bunch of conservative, nationalists had formed an irrational devotion for the EU, that they were intent on destroying democracy to impose their beliefs on the rest of us, and that they usurped the language of the left and the civil liberties movement to conceal what they were about.

In short both sides were completely misunderstood and misrepresented – the EU as being benign, liberal, progressive etc, and independence as somehow corporatist, racist or inward-looking. But that's why I campaigned on the left. Sure *'right-wing'* people misunderstood the issues too, but they misunderstood them in a good way – they thought independence would mean less regulation and less immigration which was wrong – but it meant we had their vote!

Incidentally maybe this is also a good time to deal with that point too as many people reading this may still believe it to be the true. Is it not the case that independence will mean fewer rights? less protection? less immigration and less regulation? Well maybe, possibly, but not necessarily, and this was the great misunderstanding (by both sides) of the whole campaign. The Brexit referendum was never a choice about what laws to have but about how laws were to be written. When I entered the polling booth the question in front of me didn't mention immigration, environmentalism or rights, it was about how, where and by whom legislation would be made. As I kept telling people whilst campaigning, when Britain is independent maybe we will vote for more immigration, maybe we will vote for less, that isn't my concern, my concern is that we should have a *vote* on it and as long as we were in the EU we didn't. So, our choice was essentially between a pseudo-democratic ideal or the flawed reality of representative government. Sure, I accept its possible to have a good King, or a bad Prime Minister, but overwhelmingly, across the world and throughout history, democratically elected leaders tend to reform things better and fuck things up less. So, no, greater democratic accountability did not necessarily mean fewer rights or worse environmental laws, in fact in practice it usually means the opposite.

I took the decision not to read the replies to any of my comments on the Guardian's forum, because if I had I would have exhausted and demoralised myself endlessly re-joining them. For example, let's say I was to post something like: *"Countries that govern themselves tend to be more prosperous"* there are only two types of response that will elicit:

A, *Yay, you are so clever.*

B, *Boo, you are so stupid, blah blah withering scorn.*

Ok, so neither of those conversations are particularly fruitful to engage in – we have person A's vote already and person B is never going to change their mind.

Thursday 17th September 2015

Writing in the Financial Times Jeremy Corbyn, became the most prominent left winger to capitulate: *"Labour is clear that we should remain in the EU."* It was a disavowal of everything he had previously said on the subject.

Tuesday 10th November 2015

Vicky pregnant (our second, my third). It was due in May. Life never happens at a convenient time.

Monday 4th January 2016

Back to work, back to commuting for three hours a day and back to having a nice big desktop computer for updating essays and drawing things at lunchtime and after work. I knew I had to set up as much as possible in the new year, as there would be no time once the baby arrived.

The only software I knew how to use was Autocad which is an architectural program, but it did allow me to import images, resize them, add text and export them as JPG files to post on Facebook/Twitter. It wasn't intended to be used as a graphics program, but I knew how to use it and it could do all I needed it to do.

A key weapon of the battle were memes (a simple amalgamation of image and text that could be posted and shared) and I wanted mine to have a consistent and distinctive style. I looked at the way images were displayed on Facebook and Twitter. I needed a format that was readable as soon as you scrolled onto it. If you had to click on it to read it then that was no good. It had to be like **THUD** you've got the message. I decided on a very simple format: landscape, divided into two squares, the square on the left with the face and the square on the right with the quote, and to the bottom right hand corner a two-word manifesto: 'Declare Independence'

"The opponents of EEC membership inside the Labour Party know how much more difficult it would be to foist their brand of left-wing socialism on the British people if we remain part of a community based on the principles of free enterprise and the mixed economy. We in the Conservative Party must vigorously oppose this ominous development"

Edward Heath. The Times 09.10.80

Declare independence.

I gathered the quotes and images together. First Tony Benn, then Thomas Paine, Edward Heath then Gandhi. I started to amass an array of quotes that could be used to re-join any argument I may be confronted with, and whenever I heard a good quote I quickly knocked up another meme so I could circulate it.

Donated £50 to Vote Leave

Friday January 8th
I needed a logo. A one-line idea that anyone could understand, which challenged people's assumptions by contrasting the dangers of staying with the safety of leaving. I drew up a fire escape sign, the same green colour that represents safety, made a tiny change...boom.

I see from my diary on this date that I was still revising *'Why Britain Should Be Independent.'* This essay was starting to overwhelm me.

Saturday 9th January
Ordered 20 Brexit t-shirts. 5 medium blue, 5 medium green, 5 large blue, 5 large green. (£180)

Wednesday January 13th
t-shirts done!

Thursday January 14th
Picked up stickers (£78)

Friday January 15th

I see from my diary that on this date, yes, I was *still* revising *'Why Britain Should Be Independent'*. For months, I had been staring at it for three hours a day on the train, but it was neither pamphlet, book or article. I couldn't judge it objectively any more.

I cut the sheet of stickers into rectangles of four that could be posted and put the t-shirts and stickers on my Bandcamp merchandise page. Fully expecting them to be snapped up in a few days. I never received one single order.

Wednesday 20th January
Contacted Vote Leave. Apparently, there would be a street stall in Brighton on Saturday. They put me in contact with someone called Liam Marshall.

Thursday 21st January
Liam Marshall: *'thank you so much for agreeing to help on Saturday, I just wondered if, by any chance, you had a folding table we could use?'*
SH: *'Sorry I don't, I could try Travis Perkins in the morning?'*
LM: *'That would be amazing!!! thank you so much! Let me know how much it is & I'll get it back to you!!! Thank you so much!!'*
SH: *'There is a place in New England Street that sell them. I'll pick one up Saturday morning, but I don't think I have any cloth to put over it. Do you have that? Cheers s'*
LM: *'Yes have all that. Guy who had the table had to pull out!! Thank you so much, don't know how much I appreciate it!!!'*
SH: *'No worries, it will take more than that to stop THIS campaign ... We will win! See you this Saturday, I will be wearing a Brexit T shirt!'*
LM: *'Couldn't agree more!!! The joys of teething problems lol thank you so much again'*

I ended most of my texts and emails with *"We will win!"* even though I didn't really believe it. Apparently in 1966 Alf Ramsey repeatedly said England would win the World Cup, indeed he repeated it so often it took on the air of a self-fulfilling prophecy. That's why I did it.

Friday 22nd Jan

Text from Liam: *'Hi Sebastian, really, really sorry but had a slight technical error with having the stall tomorrow. The one in Worthing is still going ahead but will have to postpone the Brighton one till next weekend!! I'm so sorry to mess you around'*

SH: *'Ok no worries, shall I still get the table?'*

LM: *'Yes if you could that would be brilliant. That way we will have one for next week'*

On this day I set up my own Facebook group *'Declare Independence'*. I had drawn up the logo in a constructivist font gleaned from Soviet posters, but although the phrase conveyed the correct sentiment, at 12 letters 'independence' was hard to use effectively in graphic design, so I didn't print it on any t-shirts.

Sunday 24th January

From this point onwards, wherever I went I always had some BREXIT stickers in my bag. At first I put them near cash machines when out pushing the pram around, but they quickly disappeared. Eventually I learned to put them where other people put them, on signs and lamp posts because these aren't cleaned that often. Ones that were high up seemed to last longer.

Friday 29th January

Texted Liam: *'Hi Liam, just checking are we still on for 10am tomorrow? Ace!'*

LM: *'Hi Sebastian I'm so sorry for the slow response!!! We are holding them in Seaford and Newhaven tomorrow. I'll be at the one at Horsham. Will have to come back to Brighton next week. I'm so sorry for these teething issues!!'*

SH: *'Cool but let's do Brighton ASAP once you have shown me the ropes I will be able to do it myself and you will be able to leave Brighton to me. Ace! We will win!'*

On this day, Karen Brady writing in the Guardian warned Brexit would have a devastating effect on British football clubs. Karen Brady was vice chairman of West Ham. My grandad used to go to the pub with Billy Bonds' dad, and I had supported them since 1979. No more.

This is an interesting example because, whilst globalisation is baffling, football has a knack of giving simple expression to complex situations. There are two ways football teams can win things – by nurturing talent or by buying talent, let's call these the *'training model'* and the *'trading model'*. There was a time when, in order to prosper, clubs had to excel at nurturing, consequently clubs had regional characteristics and particular styles of play, which the supporters would have an affinity with. But the advent of border-less markets had meant British clubs mothballed their academies and switched from training models to trading models, consequently the most successful clubs were the ones who could buy the most productive for the least, and sell the least productive for the most, to maximise revenue, to continue the process. The rules and badges were the same but the game had changed – football had become stock trading with shorts on.

As a skilful businesswoman, Brady would instinctively favour the trading model over the training model, so it was no surprise to read her defending a system which provided easy access to cheap imports, and her argument almost seemed plausible, but the trouble with it (as with so many of Remain's arguments) was that it defied the observable empirical evidence.

When West Ham relied on training rather than trading they nurtured the greatest players on planet Earth. When England won the World Cup final in 1966 all the goals were scored by West Ham players and the captain was a West Ham player, or if we look at the achievements of Brian Clough, Liverpool in the 70s or as recently as the Man United's team of 92, we see that nurturing has a proven track record of success at the highest level. How are England getting on now their biggest clubs favour the trading model? Zilch. Essentially Brady was rubbishing a model that had generated legends whilst advocating a model that had consistently failed to win fuck all, but just like every other aspect of our society, she *had* to know what she was talking about because she was a business person, right?

Sure, the trading model works for Real Madrid, but by its very nature the trading model can only ever benefit the smallest number. And no, I'm not saying football clubs should be museums – I am saying they should be successful, and the brutal reality was that as English clubs became glorified commodity traders they simply failed to replicate the success they had achieved by nurturing. So, we see, football was like a microcosm of the whole Brexit argument: when we were self-reliant we did OK (quite well in fact!) but as we became progressively reliant on cheap imports we abdicated our responsibility of making something better here and now. Generations of talented youngsters were never raised to achieve their potential so we found ourselves diminished; and all the while the executives insisted that returning to the model where local youngsters hone their skills would be a calamity.

Monday 1st February
Decided independence essay was still too broad so deleted the bit about cultural decline, but I was going down a blind alley. In the age of Twitter and memes what I needed was to break it down into a series of single-topic essays, and so that's what the independence essay became – a prototype which I

subsequently plundered to write a series of specific essays, each one of which could be used to respond to whatever was the hot topic at that point of the campaign. But it would be wrong to see it as a total failure, at the last count it had 6,100 hits on my blog, and bizarrely it carried on getting regular hits even after the vote! I don't want to bog this story down regurgitating every pre-referendum argument in this post referendum world, so here are two snippets:

"Every country needs independence for the same reason why every house needs party walls. Not because our neighbours are evil, or because we are mean, parochial or insular, but because we need to effectively organise our own lives. Conversely, being in The EU is like knocking down the party walls between our homes but on a much bigger scale – it doesn't make us more united, liberal, prosperous, safe or influential, it just turns the simplest decision into an endless technical negotiation."

"Since Britain joined the EU inequality has increased, debt has increased, pollution has increased, terrorism has increased, the NHS is diminished, the armed forces are diminished, pensions are lower, we are less democratic, manufacturing has declined, education has declined, our cities, towns and countryside are less pleasant, increasing numbers of women are subjugated, we have less privacy, unemployment has increased and GDP has halved. It's not working ... Why do we not change laws to remedy this? The answer is of course, because we have become supplicants who have abandoned the notion of governing ourselves. But now it's time to admit its failed, grow some balls and deal with our society like adults rather than palming off responsibility for decisions onto the Euro-geniuses. We don't need to believe in God or Marx or

markets, we only have to believe in ourselves, cast off fear, look up, and decide on a better future ... Unless you live in denial, closing your eyes to a mountain of empirical evidence and every lesson of history, you must accept we cannot remain subjects of an external power. Therefore, the authority of the EU over Britain is a form of government which sooner or later must end. In the name of peace let's hope its sooner rather than later."

Wednesday 3rd February
Texted Liam: *'Hi Liam, I'm up for delivering leaflets round Brighton. Feel free to post me some and I will get cracking. Cheers. S-'*

Thursday 4th February
Text from Liam: *'Hi Sebastian, so sorry for the slow reply. That would be brilliant. What's your address?'* I gave him my work address as I knew there would always be someone at the office to sign for them. That was the last contact I ever had with Liam, and though it may seem like we never sorted anything out, it was important that the first person I spoke to at Vote Leave was energised and enthusiastic. I didn't expect them to be well organised, none of us were, we were all beginners; but you will notice from our conversation that even when things weren't going right, there was never a cross word between us – it was always positive with loads of exclamation marks. Alexander the Great and Napoleon both said that morale was more important than everything else combined. Liam understood that. So, here's the next handy tip for all you would-be revolutionaries: There's no point in recriminations before you've lost, and there's no point in recriminations after you've lost.

Friday 5th February
Donated £50 to Vote Leave

Wednesday 10th February
George Monbiot essay for the Guardian: *"I'm starting to hate the EU but I will vote to stay in"*. The first of the sophisticated left-wing intellectuals to bottle it.

Monday 15th February
Donated £10 to change.org

Saturday 20th February
Having concluded his fruitless renegotiation with the EU, Dave declared he had haggled a terrific deal and confirmed the referendum would be on June 23rd. This was the formal beginning of the campaign. We had four months.

The Labour Party were going through machinations as to whether they could campaign on the same side as Cameron. I set to work on an essay entitled *'Should Labour Back Brexit?'*

Sunday 21st February
Mayor of London Boris Johnson finally declared he was backing independence. As the announcement drew near I told myself I didn't care but found myself constantly checking the phone. Surely, he couldn't bottle it? It would have been a disavowal of every opinion he had ever expressed, but you never can be sure with a politician. Was his prevarication an ideological fan dance to dramatise the inevitable? Or was he actually deliberating? After the announcement, I feigned confidence on Facebook: *"Is*

Boris backing independence because he is a man of principal? Nope, he's just scared of being on the losing side!" But his decision was not inconsequential, it gave us an advocate who was likeable, telegenic and a good communicator. And it wasn't a cowardly decision – he was putting his career on the line which is more than many others did.

Tuesday 23rd February
Whilst working I would listen to YouTube programs about Brexit to swat up on the arguments and I came across a lecture by Ruth Lea in which she observed that in opinion polls independence was regarded favourably in every category except one – the economics of it – which was strange considering there were such strong economic arguments for it. I set to work on another essay *"Is Independence Economic?"*

Owen Jones comes out for Remain. It could have been a brilliant career.

Wednesday 24th February
Bought folding table in Farringdon, £16.99, brought it back on the train.

Thursday 25th February
On this day, I set up a dedicated blog page called *'Brexit Quotes'* containing the whole arsenal of memes, so I could post one link, someone could click on it, scroll through the lot, and take whatever ones they needed. As I created more I added them to the page. It was a war, information was the ammunition, and to win you had to get the best information to the most people as early as possible. Last count 471 hits.

Next tip for all you would-be revolutionaries out there – a *'share'* is worth a thousand *'likes'*. If someone *'liked'* one of my posts that was nice, but the thing that mattered was getting the *'share'* because once the information had gone beyond my immediate circle of friends there was no telling how and where it could benefit the campaign – like a billiard ball that hits one cluster which in turn hits another, the information could then influence all manner of conversations without me having to do anything. Additionally, if someone *'shares'* some information then that is a personal recommendation which people value more highly than an image that just pops up on their news feed because some organisation paid for it to be there. So *'shares'* were referendum gold dust, and making information *'shareable'* was the holy grail of the propaganda war.

Tips for shareable memes:
1, Witty, not angry.
2, Surprise.
3, Challenge.
4, Factually correct.
5, Check spelling and grammar.

I have to admit if it was a spelling and grammar competition we would have lost. In fact, there were several times when I saw Leave memes that were so rabid or badly written I had to quickly message their authors asking for them to be taken down before they were used against us! Our use of apostrophes was especially poor.

Friday 26th February

Dan Hodges writing in the Telegraph. I will quote from it at length because its haughty dismissal of our chances was so demoralising at the time.

"Those saying we should leave Europe are infected with madness ... The Out campaign is stark raving mad ... Sky news has been busy this morning reporting the latest machinations inside the Out campaign. Nigel Farage is attempting to decapitate Douglas Carswell ... Farage is backing a group called Grassroots Out. Carswell is backing a group called Vote Leave. According to Sky, 'senior figures in UKIP have discussed trying to suspend the party's only MP over his backing for a rival group'. In just over four months' time the people of Britain will go to the polls, and they will vote – by a considerable margin – for Britain to remain in the EU. The reason why the Out campaign are going to lose is simple. The Out campaign are stark raving mad ... Insanity is not a by-product of the Out campaign. It is at the core of its offer. For out to win they know they must first destroy reason. And so, to do that they are trying to spread contagion. Not through rational argument. No, actually through fear. By simply trying to drag an entire nation through the looking glass. To convince us all to see the same upside down world they see whenever they hear the name 'Europe'"

Prescient analysis Sigmund.

Obviously, where I would like to stuff Hodges' article is the subject for another conversation in a pub some time, but here I will just make the following observation: It is one of the oldest adages in politics that divided parties don't win general elections; Hodges' error here was to think the referendum would be just like a general election, but just on a much bigger scale, and that unity was vital, in fact unity was lethal. It was the splintering of the Out campaign that won it. I will explain why later.

Another mistake Hodges made was to fixate on the leadership of the respective sides, but this was an understandable error. After all, when it came to leadership, basically they had it and we didn't! But again leadership, just like unity, was not an asset but a hindrance. It was our lack of leaders that left Remain chasing shadows, bereft of a clear figurehead to demonise they were reduced to character assassinations of Johnson and Farage, who for all their faults were hard to portray as bogeymen and didn't have a track record of failure. But did Remain have a figurehead that we could attack? Oh, boy did they – David Cameron was an opponent sent from heaven. An Eton educated millionaire who advocated spending cuts. Hated by Labour, hated by the Lib Dems, hated by the Greens and hated by half the Tory party. In the 1975 referendum Wilson had the guile to stay above the fray – not Dave! Whenever the Remain campaign hit a snag you just *knew* he was going to roll up his sleeves and drag it down a little more! I read Dan Hodges' article and my heart was in my stomach, then I looked at Cameron and thought *"there is hope"*.

Monday 29th February
On this day, I had an interview at a good architecture office in the next street in Brighton. Working 200 meters from home would have given me less commute/campaign time but it would have been handy bearing in mind Vicky was now five months pregnant. They looked at my covering letter and remarked that I lived in the next street.

"The house near the end?"

"Yes, the previous owner painted it green and white because he loved Southern Railways"

I tried to appear relaxed but our house also stood out for another reason – it was the only one in central Brighton with Vote Leave posters in the window. As soon as I got home I took them down.

Tuesday 1st March

When I do obsession, I do it properly, and from around this time till the end of the campaign I was fully in the zone. During my 90-minute commute to work I would write essays. At the cafe whilst eating I would check the papers on my phone. I would get into the office half an hour early and quickly incorporate into my blogs any revisions I felt necessary from my morning read-through. At lunch time, I would get risotto because it was the nearest quickest food stall, then I would quickly get back to my desk to post some comment on the Guardian I had been mulling over, assemble memes or correct essays. Every time I sat on the toilet I would share/retweet something on Facebook or Twitter. Then more essay writing and fact checking on the way home. As I would lie awake I would think of a killer phrase and quickly make a note of it on my phone. And as soon as my phone alarm woke me at 6 the next morning I would check the overnight developments. It was a total, total information war. I wasn't a lot of fun.

Also, it's worth noting that if Apple hadn't invented the iPhone, we would have lost.

Donated £25 to Vote Leave

Wednesday 2nd March

From my diary: *"I'm really scared, I'm having trouble concentrating, it started again yesterday, I may not be able to do this job much longer"*

I had recently received a blow to the back of my head and at work I was finding it difficult to concentrate on technical problems. Eventually it was diagnosed as concussion which gradually dissipated but for a while I was very frightened that I may not be able to support my family, and might even become a burden to them. I managed to cover up my difficulties by working late.

But it wasn't all despondency, hope came from the most unlikely source: Lord Rose, head of the Remain campaign suggested in evidence to the Treasury Select Committee, that any restrictions on EU migrants would mean *"the price of labour will, frankly, go up."* What an idiot. What a gift … *'vote Brexit and get a pay rise!'* If ever you wondered how much intelligence you need to sit in the House of Lords there's your answer. Strangely enough we didn't hear much more from Lord Rose for the rest of the campaign.

Thursday 3rd March

On this day, I published my first mini-essay *'Is Independence Economic?'* Again, I don't want to bog this story down regurgitating every pre-referendum argument in this post-referendum world, but briefly it made three observations:

1, Independent countries tend to have twice the GDP and half the unemployment of Eurozone countries (USA, Canada, Australia, New Zealand, India, South Korea, Japan, Norway, Greenland, Iceland, Switzerland etc)

2, There is a general correlation between EU integration and economic decline.

3, I contrasted Britain's pre '73 prosperity with its steady decline afterwards.

It was ok but maybe I should have simplified it into two or three even smaller essays, also having a cover image of America's founding fathers probably made it look fusty and switched people off. At the count, it had 361 hits.

Anyway, I posted it on my Facebook wall and a friend called Mike, who I had performed alongside at various poetry slams, responded to it by posting a link to a conversation between Paul Mason and Yanis Varoufakis where they discussed how disastrous Brexit would be.

Tuesday 8th March

So, the whole thing was basically one big information war and more than anywhere else it was fought out on Facebook. This was because the format of Facebook was more conversational than Twitter, whilst unlike the newspapers, TV and radio there was no editorial barrier you had to get past before joining in. It was the great level playing field – you could just pick up your phone and rant to the world and his dog all day long, either under your own name or via some dedicated page/group.

The *'Stronger In'* page on Facebook was the main Remain page and got huge numbers of *'likes'* and *'shares'*. (For a while this was actually the best place to post stuff as they had such big audiences, but the administrators got wise to this and blocked me.) By contrast there was a plethora of Brexit pages on Facebook ranging from the eccentric to the conscientious to the downright insane: *'Liberal Youth*

*for Leave' 'Vote out for a Socialist Europe' 'Goodbye EU'
'Green Leaves' 'United Patriots' 'Brexit News' 'Vote
Leave Derbyshire' 'Luvvies For Leave'* etc etc. So, the
'Stronger In' page had stuff that was authoritative
and professionally put together with a big
circulation, whereas the Brexit pages tended to be
niche groups that were more amateur. But there were
one or two fringe Remain groups too like *'Healthier
In'* or *'Scientists for the EU'* and on this day, I posted
on their pages rebutting some of their points. I
promptly got another message from Mike:

*'Yo Seb – I deleted your 'posts' on Healthier In because
the comments section is for discussion of the issues not
lazy link-spamming'*

I replied: *'coolsville, no hard feelings sir'*

He replied: 👍

Intelligent, creative, handsome, likeable, hard-
working, professional, confident, charismatic,
articulate and worst of all well-organised, Mike was
exactly the sort of person you wouldn't want to see
in the opposing team. Worse still he had spotted the
problem with the Remain campaign and was clearly
intent on doing something about it. I wrote above
that it was actually an advantage that the Brexit
campaign was fragmented (26th February) this was
because it meant our information was targeted at
specific groups with specific interests and was
written in a variety of ways that each particular
audience could relate to. By contrast the Remain side
had only one voice. It was a professional voice, and it
was an authoritative voice but it also came across as
official. Their warnings of a Brex-pocalypse often had
the air of a lecture, and their EU-logies tended to
come across as adverts, whereas however amateur

the Brexit propaganda was, it was clearly written by real people who weren't being paid to write it. That's what Mike had spotted – the Remain campaign wasn't diverse enough so he was obviously setting up his own niche groups. Clever.

Thursday 10th March
On this day, I published *'Should Labour back Brexit?'* Last count 798 hits. Again, there's no point reproducing the whole argument here. Money quote:

"When they [Labour] observe the working class political activism sweeping the country do they twig it's what they have waited for all their lives? How could Labour get such an easy decision so wrong? How could they be so naive as to take Cameron's side? What suckers they are, that even now, on the biggest issue of all, they are with Tony Blair rather than Tony Benn? And how could they be so credulous as to think the EU gives us more progressive legislation than we could write for ourselves? For Labour, to campaign against independence isn't just morally wrong – it's an act of baffling political suicide."

Had a delivery of leaflets to the office from Vote Leave.

Friday 11th March
The next day would be the first ever Brexit street stall in Brighton so this is a good point to say something about Brighton and what I do.

I write songs and poems and I perform them at open mic nights, and since moving to Brighton I had made contact with lots of the local promoters and performers and played at various events. I hadn't done much for a while because of the baby, but it was always my intention that once established in the town I would sort out my live act and get on the circuit. Now if you don't know much about what type of town Brighton is, it's, well, *different* from other towns. Brighton is the most right-on, left-wing, drop-out centre in England. And being smaller than London it has a village feel, people know one another, the networks are more intimate and you bump into acquaintances on the street all the time. And who were the most pro-EU people in this, the most pro-EU town in England? You guessed it – the people at open mic nights! So, by coming out as Brexit I was effectively closing the door on that whole scene. Of course, all promoters will say they are cool with political material, and of course they advocate free expression of what you really believe; but that is always on the understanding that what you are going to express is an anti-Thatcher bore-a-thon about social justice. To be Brexit was unfashionable, but to have a Brexit sticker on your guitar at an open mic night in Brighton was to be an untouchable. I didn't even bother asking for gigs any more, the Remain side had been so successful at portraying my views as a type of sociopathic mental illness I just presumed I was hated, but at a certain point you have to put the badge on.

This is a sticker that was common on Brighton lamp posts at the time.

So, while we can argue about which side was really progressive there is no question which side *appeared* the most progressive. Passing themselves off as enlightened and outward-looking modernists was a hugely successful tactic for Remain because it pre-emptively silenced so many counter- arguments.

Saturday 12th March

The lowest point is the first step. I hesitated at the door, opened it, carried the wall paper pasting table outside and leant it against the wall, then I rolled out the purple wheelie suitcase packed with leaflets pens and badges, I mumbled something to Vicky kissed her on the cheek and started plodding down the street.

I was wearing my scruffiest clothes, the important thing was to counter everyone's assumption that we were spivs or racists so I wore an old pair of shoes with holes in them that had string as laces, my jeans were ankle-swingers with paint on and my cardigan was my DIY top also with paint and glue stains, I wore my old woolly bobble hat (blue and white stripes – Brighton colours) and my Brexit t-shirt. Every step, I felt that behind every window people were looking at me aghast, and as I dragged the suitcase through the streets I felt like my heart was in my stomach.

At New Road, I bumped into a young man with a Vote Leave badge, he said his name was Christian. I seem to remember he was a Conservative Councillor. At the corner of New Road and North Street there was a chipboard hoarding because the shop behind was being fitted out. It was a really nice backdrop because it had a sort of revolutionary style painting on it. I put the table there, on the corner against the hoarding, put the cloth over it and got the leaflets out.

A guy with a beard turned up, about the same amount of grey hair as me, but nowhere near as grumpy as me, quite chirpy in fact considering the task ahead! We chatted briefly, and it quickly became evident that he wasn't just another nutter, and that he completely understood what we had to do and why we had to do it. He had brought his own leaflets which were better than mine because they explained how much money each household would save by leaving. He said his name was Paul. Someone else called Nigel turned up, a conservative councillor called Daisy and also an amazing lady called Vicki who said she had once stood as an independent. I think out of everyone there I was the only one who had zero experience of campaigning.

So, I picked up some leaflets and found a spot to hand them out. The leaflets weren't brilliant, there was one decent one called 'Five Positive Reasons to Leave' and another terrible one about how the money we send to Greece could fix all the pot holes in our roads, which as a non-driver would have left me unmoved.

5 *positive* reasons to Vote Leave and take back control

Europe yes, EU no

Ok so I was ready to go, but how to campaign? The first couple of things I said as I offered leaflets to people seemed so futile, I felt like I was just mouthing words that drifted off in the breeze. People would reply *"NO!"* or *"IN!"* The animosity was palpable, and because we set up very early before there were many people about, lots of the time I was just standing awkwardly in an empty street feeling like an eyesore.

It takes a while to find your own voice and no one can teach you how to do it. Paul would say *"Five positive reasons to leave the EU?"* or *"See how much you can save!"* and he would hold the leaflets out in front of people. Vicki would sidle up to people and engage them in a friendly conversation. But that didn't feel right for me, I was a songwriter so I wanted killer phrases that gave people the vision in the smallest possible number of words. The longer I tried, the clearer my voice got, I started to annunciate better and my phrases became more cogent: *"declare independence – it always works"* … *"Independence works"* … *"I AM REVOLTING!"* … *"Brex-terminate Cameron"* (I had to make sure Christian and Daisy didn't hear that one) … The high street got busier, I learned to turn my head as people walked past so my mouth was always pointing at their ears, so even if they didn't take a leaflet they still got the message. And every time a person took a leaflet, as I thanked them I felt a glimmer of hope and heard a little more optimism in my own voice.

I had a few conversations but not many which was a failure on my part because whenever I did I felt I gave people a new perspective on the issue that just wasn't appearing in the main stream media. I never really got rid of heaps of leaflets because I offered them rather than pushing them on people, but I got a message out; and just our prescience, just the fact that we were there, doing it in the most pro-EU city in England was important. Several times people would shout back *"Wrong town!"* but Brighton was the *right* town – nothing would have been less productive than campaigning in a UKIP stronghold!

One thing you learn doing street campaigning is not to get embroiled in conversations with people who agree with you because that isn't winning any votes. But one punter showed up who was definitely worth talking to. He didn't need any persuading – he had a badge on his jacket saying something like 'No to the EEC' and we chatted for a while about when we had seen Tony Benn speak, he gave us his email address, and said his name was Peter.

A homeless guy on a bike came along and said his name was Scouse John. He looked at the pile of Brexit t-shirts. I hadn't sold any so I said he could have one. He promised to wear it every day till the vote. Part of me hopes he didn't.

Some Remain people turned up and campaigned right next to us. They were determined to get right in our faces with the sort of righteous contempt that was a common feature of their campaign. If I was talking to someone they would barge in, but I always kept it jovial, and eventually they moved on to the other end of New Road.

As the day went on I managed to give out a few badges and stickers and even sold a couple of t-shirts! Eventually it was time to pack up and I asked Paul what he thought. He seemed very chipper and said that now it was up and running the important thing was to do it every Saturday as a regular thing so it would gain momentum and become easier to organise. Every time I met Paul he would say something that was:

A, Very simple

B, Obviously correct

C, Something no one else had thought of saying.

I said that next Saturday would be a problem as my mum was getting married (bloody inconvenient!) but that yes, every Saturday thereafter.

It was time to go. I was hoarse, exhausted and slightly sun burned, but something felt strange, there seemed to be something in the air. I found myself wanting to stay a few more minutes to hand out just a few more leaflets, I didn't want it to stop. For the first time I scented victory, and by the time I hauled the stuff back along New Road the Remain people had gone.

Thursday 17th March
Looking back through my diary it's surprising how much other stuff I was attempting to do at this same time. Maybe I wasn't as committed as I thought, or maybe I just took on too much, but on this day, I paid for the final masters for an album called Tascam I had been working on for the last 18 months. My problem is that I tend to turn every little job into a grand project, and I had been pissing about with Tascam for about 8 months longer than I should have, but the good thing about the referendum was that there was a deadline – on June 23rd it would be over, so we couldn't piss about. It was obvious it would end in a frenzy.

Friday 18th March
Still no word from the Brighton job interview so I put the Vote Leave posters back up in the windows.

Saturday 19th March
The Brighton campaign was suspended this day owing to the fact that, this was the day I walked my mother down the aisle. The music as we entered was *'In My Life'* by the Beatles. Everyone was there, everything was perfect. I gave a nice speech. Didn't mention Brexit.

Monday 21st March

My Declare Independence page on Facebook had barely any followers. Facebook was suggesting other groups to me all the time, why wasn't my group being suggested to other people? I didn't need thousands of followers but I did need a respectable number to feed arguments into the general conversation and crucially I needed followers who were themselves opinion formers who shared information. I started paying Facebook to promote specific posts.

Its clever how this aspect of Facebook works – it allows you to do a large number of very cheap promotions. You just select the post, decide how much you want to spend, tag it, select age/gender of recipients and press 'Go'. Then you check what got the most shares to help target the next post better. The tags I used were: *Feminism, LGBT, social equality, gender equality, socialism* and *environmentalism*. By polling day my page had 522 followers but every £5 promotion got it on about 1500 people's time lines, and *that's* why Facebook is worth billions – right now it's where the future is being decided.

Saturday 26th March

The second Brexit corner, I reluctantly dragged myself through town, got to the spot and stood there on my own feeling sorry for myself, wondering if anyone else would turn up. I hesitated. I really didn't feel like it. I decided that if no one else turned up in the next five minutes I would take a cab to George Street to campaign with the Hove group. Part of me was even half-hoping that no one would turn up so I would have an excuse for quitting. A tall guy with dark hair, walked up, crushed my hand and said he was Ian. Ok so the second Brexit corner was on. We unpacked the stuff. Paul and someone called Sasha turned up too and we got to work. There was no longer a chipboard hoarding on the corner, the restaurant was now open and manager came straight out and said that we had to move because he didn't want his business to be associated with us. We moved further up the street and set the table up in an alcove. A few feet away there was a doorway which was the entrance to the offices of the Brighton Fringe Festival. The doorway was a bit hidden so when lost looking performers came ambling along I would direct them to the Fringe office.

Predictably it wasn't long before one of the management came out and said we had to move. We had a legal right to be there and we weren't obstructing any fire escape, but like the restaurant owner, they just didn't want to be associated with us.

Hannah arrived for work at the Fringe office. I knew her from the year before when I had put on my one-man show. I explained to her we would be happy to move in about half an hour as soon as the rain eased off. Hannah was totally cool, she may even have remembered that the previous year I had donated the profits from my show to the Brighton Fringe which is a registered charity.

Hopefully this was another tiny way in which we detoxified our image. Gave another t-shirt to some homeless guy. They weren't selling.

I believe this was the first day I met John Kapp, a man of about 75 who turned up to help. He had his own leaflets that were better than ours because they had 'NHS' on the front and contrasted the expanding EU budget with the austerity being applied to public services. He gave us some and I gave him a t-shirt. We swapped email addresses.

Half way through we were running low on some leaflets so I said I would dash home and fetch some more. As I ran back I used the Siri voice recognition system on my phone to send Vicky a text letting her know I was popping back:

"Hey baby, just coming back for some more stuff x x"

At the door, Vicky seemed surprised to see me. Siri had sent it to Brexit Vicki rather than wife Vicky!

Many of the people I spoke to were surprisingly uninformed or confused about the issues, which was understandable for two main reasons:

1, It's a complex subject.

2, In the heat of battle vast amounts of *'information'* was being circulated that was designed to confuse rather than enlighten and much of the propaganda (admittedly from both sides) was unnecessarily emotive.

Every time I set up the stall I felt like a loser, and wanted to be anywhere except where I was, but just like the first Brexit corner, when it was time to pack up I didn't want it to end, and as one by one we returned to our lives I always wanted to do a few more minutes and give out just a few more leaflets.

Wednesday 30th March
I realised the most important document on my iPad was missing. The *'Lyrics'* file containing every song writing idea I have ever had, just wasn't there anymore. But it should be ok because I had backed it up to the iCloud.

Thursday 31st March
At lunchtime I emailed David Smith, Economics Editor of the Times. The LSE had issued a paper warning of the dangers of Brexit, Leave campaigners claimed that because the LSE is funded by the EU, it was feigning impartiality and David Smith, who I much admired, had defended the LSE.

Dear David Smith,
I have read your column every week for several years now, and noted your postscript this week regarding the referendum.
I think there are essentially two ways of evaluating the advantages or disadvantages of a choice – to hypothesise about what might happen or to observe what did happen when a similar choice was made in the past. Of the two methods, I would always favour the observational as it involves interpretation of facts that exist rather than speculation about a future that doesn't.
The problem I have with the LSEs statistics is not that they are partial, but that they are hypothesising that Britain would be the first country in history to declare independence then

subsequently become poorer. If we regard the history of countries that declared independence there seems to be very little empirical evidence to justify this claim, even for countries like India for whom independence was a much riskier venture.

Please don't feel under any obligation to reply, I appreciate you are very busy and this a subject that we will all be pretty sick of by June 23rd. Keep up the great writing!

Yours sincerely S-

More leaflets were delivered to the office. I stored the boxes under my desk and I brought home one box of 1,000 every day, then at home I stashed them in the kitchen. But the piles of boxes in the kitchen were getting bigger and Vicky was getting concerned Jnr was climbing on them. The campaign was encroaching more and more on home life – literally! Another problem was that water had started dripping through the kitchen ceiling whenever it rained. I promised Vicky I would sort it out as soon as the referendum was over. Sometimes, I felt that overthrowing the government was the easy bit, and that the real achievement was marrying someone prepared to stand by me as I did it.

Reply from David Smith!

Sebastian, Thanks for your e-mail. You are right to say that lack of precedent is a source of uncertainty in projections of this kind. Only Greenland has left Europe – the EEC. However, leaving the EU is very different from achieving independence from a colonial master. And there have been plenty of examples where, even in those circumstances,

countries have experienced prolonged periods of
economic decline after independence.
Regards David Smith

Obviously, I knew about Greenland already and the whole point was that there were heaps of precedents, and that the EU was absolutely acting like a colonial master. But although I disagreed I respectfully disagreed. He was a busy man who could never be accused of being poorly informed so I spared him the rejoinder. During the whole campaign, David Smith was virtually the only decent economist I came across who favoured Remain despite not being an interested party. Anatole Kaletsky was the other. The economists who called it right were Irwin Stelzer, Larry Elliott, Ruth Lea, Patrick Minford, Roger Bootle and David Blake.

Friday 1st April
It was about this time that we received the notorious referendum booklet. Designed and printed by the Government at a cost to the taxpayer of about £9,500,000. My heart sank the moment I saw it because it meant their campaign was up and running, they were punching and we were getting hit. I leafed through it despondently, it was an anthology of all their best arguments. I felt our votes draining away in their thousands. A document of shameful mendacity, it masqueraded as impartial factual information whilst employing every conceivable device to deliver partial, emotive, fact-free propaganda.

I started grinding my teeth, pacing around the room. I picked it up again then put it down again. I wanted to film it being burnt or photograph it hanging from the toilet roll holder, but Vicky had a better idea, she said I would have to write an essay against it: *"if it wasn't for what you had told me, I would read this, accept it, and vote remain."* What a project to have in your in tray! Overseen by the Prime Minister and Chancellor, written by a top team of civil servants and political strategists, and designed to carry the full authority of HM Government. A lot of people had spent a lot of time and money making it persuasive; I had a phone, an iPad and a few train journeys to rebut it. But she was right, we couldn't just ignore or dismiss Cameron's booklet.

So, another grand project to keep me awake at night, but from this inauspicious beginning and Vicky's good advice emerged probably the best bit of campaigning I did.

Saturday 2nd April
The third Brexit corner. This was when a serious strategic mistake got established at the stall. In order to be more evenly distributed around the nearby street corners, I started standing further away from the table and left others to oversee the collecting of email addresses. At the end of the day I didn't notice that there were very few new email addresses and that those we did have were often illegible. I was so busy shouting clever slogans on the other side of the street I completely failed to notice this was a problem. It cost us hundreds of votes.

My abiding memory of the third Brexit corner was seeing John Kapp across the road in his Brexit t-shirt handing out leaflets. Beside him, propped up against a bollard was a sign he had made himself. Somehow, I ended up looking after this sign and I still have it at home today under the stairs. Ian didn't like it because of its amateurism, and Ian was probably right, but still my heart leaps whenever I see it. If there is one physical object on planet Earth that is the embodiment of why we won it is John Kapp's Vote Leave sign.

Whilst handing out leaflets I bumped into an old friend, a Japanese lady who was married to a really nice Austrian guy. It was awkward. If I had spotted her walking up the street I would have hidden till she had gone past. Hopefully she knew me well enough to disbelieve what everyone said about us.

Sunday 3rd April
Went to the Apple Store, they were no help. The backup that I had saved to the iCloud a hundred times just wasn't there. They said all I could do was phone up the help desk. This was the absolutely the last thing in the world I needed – to be sent on a wild goose chase calling some customer service

department in Ireland. I checked my work computer, I had a version from December 2013 but apart from that nothing. I was numb with grief – years of work was gone.

That night I chanced playing one last gig – Vapour Vox – after that I never dared show my face on the music/poetry circuit again. That career was over, but hey, no one liked my songs much anyway.

Monday 4th April

When campaigning on Brexit corner we never had much time to discus with one another what we were doing or how we should do it. Several attempts had been made to arrange a meet up with everyone on the email list but I have to admit these were amateurish to the point of being farcical. Various emails proposing various locations on various dates would fly round, each one to a different set of people and when one person couldn't make this or that date the whole process would begin again. We couldn't even get together to begin to organise ourselves!

When arranging meetings, you have a choice: one with everyone that never happens, or one that happens that's not with everyone. I suggested that instead of trying to get the world and his dog to the same meeting we should just propose a time and date and see who turned up. So, we decided on the Sidewinder pub in Kemptown, Thursday evening.

Tuesday 5th April

Potential catastrophe. The Panama Papers scandal had just broken, revealing to the internet the names of thousands of people who had hidden their wealth in secret offshore funds. The previous day Iceland's PM Sigmundur Gunnlaugsson had been forced to resign, and on this day, it emerged that David Cameron's late father had set up such a fund which Dave had profited from. This was serious. If the scandal brought him down then the Remain campaign might have been led by someone popular! To my huge relief Dave rode it out.

Thursday 7th April
Donated £100 to Vote Leave
Straight after work I made my way to the pub. It was a bit noisy so I grabbed a table in the beer garden, Paul turned up, then Peter and Ian. Yes, we were all white middle-aged men but it was curious how different we all were.

Paul was a libertarian. At one point, he had been a UKIP candidate and for a brief period a member of the Conservative party, but he was too ideologically driven for the petty compromises of party membership. He had set up an on-line radio show called Radio Free UK and had made stacks of YouTube videos with tips on how to campaign. But don't let me give you the impression he was some type of crank, his understanding of why we had to win and how we should do it was comprehensive. He took his copy of Cameron's booklet out of his bag: *"We all have to read this because these are the arguments that people will say to us"*. Another phrase I remember him saying: *"the leaflets aren't doing any good on the table"*.

Ian was a no-nonsense Scot, and had been part of the SNP back when they actually believed in independence. He looked at the menu and wondered aloud why everything had to come with salad? Without any fuss, Ian became the most indispensable member of the group, by sheer force of relentlessly turning up again and again.

It was impossible not to like Peter. Proper Labour, trade unionist, anti EEC and absolutely driven by principle. He made it clear that he wasn't anti-immigration and that if it was an anti-immigration group he wanted no part of it. It was a good call to get that established from the outset, after all there were 9 weeks of campaigning left and I was already sick of people thinking it was a vote about what immigration policy to have! But the point is we had to keep the conversation about what to do rather than why we were doing it, or else right at the beginning we would have started arguing and fallen apart.

Ian spoke about the need to get a big placard to really announce the presence of the stall. I nodded, but being sheepish about Brexit I felt happy to just plod on with my jobs and leave the placard to him. When Ian finally did sort out a big banner he was proved spectacularly right, it really helped. It cost us votes that I didn't support his idea from the outset.

Peter spoke about how we needed to concentrate on recruitment so that there would be so many people handing out leaflets it would send a real message. I remember when he said this I was scared he was going to bring his fist down on the table! Again, I nodded but didn't offer much help other than what I was doing already. This was another mistake by me, because again he was on to something I hadn't spotted – we were concentrating on winning votes all by ourselves when with nine weeks to go the priority should have been to build a big team.

We spoke about leafleting houses and I said I would get a map together. They spoke about doing it in Whitehawk – the area around the football stadium, but although we all delivered leaflets individually the Brighton Brexiteers never got around to doing it as a group.

It may sound like a shambles but it wasn't, because now we felt like a team, and it's fair to say the Brighton Brexiteers never really existed till that night. After Ian and Peter left I remarked to Paul how different we all were. He replied: *"that's why it had to be you that started it – the group wouldn't have coalesced around something set up by Labour or Tory or UKIP, Green or Anarchist."* Again, Paul spotted something that never occurred to me!

Anyway, I can't remember much else about our conversation that night but I can remember what we didn't talk about. No one ever asked *"do you think we will win?"* I suppose to maintain morale we had all adopted an unspoken understanding to not ask that question. Remain had done such a good job of portraying their victory as inevitable we were all privately resigned to embittered defeat. So why did we bother? I'm not sure, I suppose it was because it was unthinkable not to.

Friday 8th April
Interview Battersea. God knows what I was thinking of going to interviews at this time. They liked me and the money would have been good, but in the middle of the campaign with a pregnant wife it would have been insanity to change employers. On the train, I watched Paul's YouTube video debunking Cameron's booklet and plagiarised the best bits for my essay.

On this date, I published *'Was Independent Britain Less Liberal?'* In it I contrasted Britain's key political acts in the 40 years before and after joining the EEC. So on the one hand we have: confronting fascism, setting up the NHS, Welfare State and green belt, passing the Clean Air Act, the Race Relations Act, the Equal Pay Act, the decriminalisation of homosexuality and the abolition of the death penalty – whilst on the other hand we have the Thatcher privatisations, Thatcher's signing of The Single European Act, Big Bang, Maastricht, joining the ERM, the Lisbon treaty, the Criminal Justice Act, giving independence to the Bank of England, the bailing out of the banks, the subsequent austerity, and the current deregulation of planning law. My general point was that the post '73 reforms were about liberalising trade and commerce, so we went from being a liberal society to a neoliberal one. Last count 327 hits.

Saturday 9th April
Brexit corner. From this point to the end of the campaign I made my spot the entrance to the alley that lead to the South Laines as three lots of pavement intersected there, so I was always busy. A man waiting to cross the road heard me, walked up and said: *"I should push you under a bus"*. That ended up number two of the top five insults I received.

Illustration – John Kapp and Darren Grimes.

Later on, my dad turned up from London unexpectedly and asked if I could knock off early, I said I was sorry I couldn't but that he should go back to our house, have some tea, and spend some time with his grandson till I had finished. He said he thought it was wrong that I was shouting *"Brex-terminate Cameron"* as it made it about personalities not policies. That was a fair point, but the one argument that automatically floored the socialists and environmentalists and the *'progressives'* was that they were with Cameron. Could they really denounce austerity one day and stand with him the next? He was our shield, our mascot, our trump card.

Monday 11th April
Published *'Cameron's Leaflet Debunked'*. Here is the opening paragraph:

"This leaflet will be studied by political scientists for years to come as a textbook example of how to lose a referendum. What a gift to independence campaigners like myself that the opposition should hand us a concise summary of their main arguments to knock down one by one. Just crit these ten pages sentence by sentence and we've won the argument. Easy!"

It's usually difficult to structure long essays but this one was fairly simple because I just took their booklet as the basis for what I wrote, working through it sentence by sentence. This meant that the final essay was long, but that was less of a problem in this instance because people could just dip into it as a reference source to check whichever counter-argument interested them.

The hardest thing about the Leaflet Debunked essay was that to write it I had to swot up on the most boring technicalities imaginable. Who cares about the difference between an import tariff and an export tariff? You don't, I don't, no one does, but you *have* to know in order to argue against a technocratic institution, this was another clever strategy of the EU.

The US constitution is simple because it's about liberty and the pursuit of happiness, the EU constitution is a labyrinth because it's about binding people together. And if people don't want to be bound together they are told that peace, happiness and prosperity are dependent upon various institutions and technicalities that no one can even name, but which assuredly safeguard us from unimaginable horror. Do you understand all the technicalities? If not it's assumed you are not entitled to dissent, so at a stroke those who can criticise goes from 100% of the population to 0.01% of the population. And even if you are one of the few who can grasp the issues, it becomes very hard to explain your misgivings with any passion or clarity. And that is how vision-less technicians incubate their failure as leaders, and for requiring me to read up on bilateral trade agreements alone, the EU deserves to burn in hell fire.

The essay consistently got traffic and by polling day had received about 6,980 views on my WordPress site.

Wednesday 13th April

Latest quote from Jean-Claude Juncker: *"when it gets serious you have to lie."* I knocked up the meme straight away...

"When it becomes serious, you have to lie"

- Jean-Claude Juncker

Declare independence.

Saturday 16th April

No Brexit corner this week, as the Handleys had to go to a wedding in Devon. Bloody weddings! A big concern though was what if Vicky went into labour while we were out of town? Jnr had come five weeks early so realistically we had to be prepared for our daughter to arrive at any moment! As time went on and the baby didn't come we became more and more anxious.

Monday 18th April

On this day Chancellor of the Exchequer, George Osborne staged a press conference claiming that Brexit would make every household in Britain £4,300 per year worse off by 2030. This claim was based on the assumption that it would make our economy 6% smaller.

What? In 14 years our economy would be 6% smaller than today? But that hasn't happened to any major economy in 300 years! – except Germany after 1938.

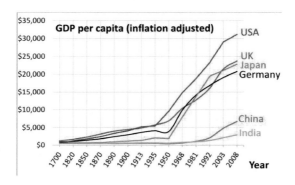

Ahh no, that was just the impression that Osborne *wanted* you to get, actually the claim was that we would be 6% poorer than if we had chosen to remain.

Obviously, any serious economist making a prediction about things in 14 years' time would go out of their way to stress the high degree of uncertainty involved in this sort of thing, and would at least acknowledge awareness of alternative forecasts that predicted otherwise. Not Osborne. The Treasury had conducted a *'Gravity'* model which we can picture as a model of the Newtonian Solar System. The assumption was that the EU is the radiant Sun and that the countries most deeply integrated (closest) benefit most from membership.

Thus, Italy and France would be like Mercury and Venus and glow with prosperity whilst Norway and Switzerland would be out in the cold around Pluto somewhere. So, Osborne's theory was that we would end up like Uranus – but there were several holes in it!

1, The reduction of UK exports to the EU from 54% in 2006 to 44% in 2015 was inconsistent with their model.

2, They assumed that despite being the 5th largest economy we wouldn't be able to negotiate trade deals with anyone.

3, Greenland's rapid growth after it left the EU was inconsistent with their model.

4, His report assumed there would be no political response to any short-term shock.

5, He was confusing GDP per household with household income.

6, He was assuming that if we remained our budget contributions wouldn't exponentially increase.

Their gravity model was entirely based on an assumption for which there was no empirical evidence – that there was a direct correlation between EU membership and a prospering economy. The same economic model would predict that Britain would be better off joining the Euro, that every country in the world would be better off joining the EU, and that an independent Scotland's trade with the rest of the UK would reduce by 80%. They were making it up. And if the gravity model was so cool then as well as conducting one for our trade with the 27 EU member states, why not compare this to a gravity model of our trade with the 109 non-EU member states?

So, George *'Crystal Ball'* Osborne had no plan in place for the biggest political event of his life that was about to happen in 66 days' time, but he was happy to pontificate about how the economy would be in 2030! If ever you wondered how numerate you have to be to be chancellor there's your answer. I think I could take any one of my bosses, stick them in 11 Downing Street and they would make a decent fist of it. Nick Campbell, Alain Bouvier, Simon Sturgis, give any of them Osborne's job and they would do ok. But could George Osbourne oversee a building project? Maybe, but I wouldn't bet on it standing up 14 years later.

Also by this point I was pretty much fed up of hearing the phrase *"but Europe has given us peace"* so I began collecting together my arguments against that.

Thursday 21st April
8am interview Galliard Homes Canary Wharf.

Again, idiotically, in the middle of the campaign and with Vicky pregnant I agreed to do an interview. I was just exhausting myself in a flurry of commitments when the most important thing was to think clearly.

At the interview, I asked who the project architects were:

GH: Rolfe Judd

SH: Rupert Anderson?

GH: He's project architect.

SH: I was in a punk band with him 18 years ago!

Strange how the past can crop up. Didn't get the job.

Barack Obama was visiting Britain. A month earlier he had said that the catastrophe unfolding in Libya was in part down to Cameron being *"distracted"*. It was an odd lapse of protocol for such a sure-footed politician but on this day, he certainly made amends for it. Speaking next to Cameron at the Foreign Office he said that if Britain left the EU and then tried to negotiate a trade deal with the US, we would find ourselves *"at the back of the queue"* Cameron could not have asked for any more from his guest.

There must have been high fives at Remain HQ. It would be hard to imagine a more ringing endorsement for their cause or more withering scorn for ours, and all in a crisp unforgettable metaphor about a uniquely British activity: queuing; worst of all, it was breezily delivered by the most authoritative and respected statesman on planet Earth. It was a coup for Remain.

I think Obama is probably the greatest president since Reagan, but for those four words for me his name will always reside in ignominy. He lived in an independent nation, why shouldn't we? The USA enjoyed government of the people, for the people, by the people, why shouldn't we? Essentially Obama was disavowing the very principles for which the USA was supposed to stand, and for what? To prevent clearly necessary change to a dysfunctional political system designed to insulate the powerful from the electorate.

There are two types of nation in the world: either the people tell the government what to do, or the government tell the people what to do. At this pivotal moment in our history which side was Obama on? Did he stand by the founding principles of the USA? or maintain a discreet silence? or at least speak with qualified circumspection? No. He employed all his rhetorical skill to belittle us into accepting supplication, and in so doing demeaned his office.

We all make mistakes but for Mr. Change to stand at the threshold of a new age and actually campaign against the powerful being answerable to voters is not just a technical error of judgement – some decisions are so big and so wrong that the stain is indelible.

Saturday 23rd April
Brexit corner. A guy in a camouflage jacket turned up and we started talking about anarcho-socialism and (as usual) Tony Benn. The thing about these so-called *'fringe nutters'* is that when you take the trouble to actually listen to them, so many are so well informed – he could have taught history! We exchanged email addresses. He said his name was Wayne.

Wayne was the last significant addition to the group, so let's spend a minute looking at the make-up of the Brighton operation to see what it tells us. There were various semi-detached affiliates like John Kapp, Darren Grimes, Nigel Furness and Anne Meadows who knew the Brighton group but mostly campaigned apart from it. Then there was an inner circle of six people: Vicki (Independent) Paul (Libertarian) Wayne (Anarchist) Ian (SNP) Peter (Socialist) and me (Eco-atheist) and it was a self-organising syndicate with no leaders and no followers. People accused us of being *'far-right'* but actually the Brighton Brexiteers was a classic example of an Anarchist collective!

There was a bit more argy-bargy with Labour/Remain People, but Peter saw them off with his subsidiarity booglarizer.

Whereas we were a disparate collection of people who came together for the referendum, the Remain campaign in Brighton was basically the Green Party or the Labour Party wearing *'IN'* t-shirts - they were formed of pre-existing groups. So, when Remain campaigned in Brighton they tended to cluster on one street corner and really dominate it whereas we would meet up then straight away spread out with one person on each corner. This meant that most of the time each of us was operating in total isolation, so we were much more prone to being demoralised than the Remainers. I think this is why Remain tended to be over confident whilst we tended to be bloody minded pessimists.

Why did remain always operate in clusters? Why didn't they put one person on each corner like us? Could it be that even the way we stood in the street subconsciously reflected our respective political positions? They clustered together whereas we were not afraid to stand alone?

Monday 25th April
On this date, the Guardian released their unfunny film in which Patrick Stewart played a bigoted right wing Prime Minister, who swivel-eyed and foam flecked with rage demands his cabinet answer *"What has the European Convention on Human Rights ever done for us?"*

From the first few sentences it's obvious we're in for a sneer-a-thon, and sure enough the cabinet coolly point out a succession of heavenly reforms the ECHR *'gave us'* which made us truly human, until stupefied with rage Prime Minister Bigot spontaneously combusts in defeat.

Maybe they could have laid it on a bit thicker? Maybe they could have given Patrick Stewart a little Hitler moustache and have him goose-step around the room like Basil Fawlty? Or possibly they could have shown the cabinet feeding starving refugees as Stewart fucked a polar bear? But no – these guys were too classy for that.

I was going to write *'obviously, the ECHR is different to the EU'* but actually to most people it's not obvious at all, in fact what's *really* obvious is that by throwing this propaganda grenade into the middle of the referendum campaign the Guardian were hoping to get people to conflate the two, so their film would appear to be a microcosm of the entire referendum debate, with calm outward-looking people vanquishing hysterical hatred with cold facts. So on this day I began my next essay *'Did Europe Give Us Human Rights?'* After all it was important to me that calm outward-looking people triumph over hysteria with facts.

Saturday 30th April

Brexit corner was different this week. Chris Grayling, Leader of the House and prominent Vote Leave campaigner was coming to Brighton to have a picture taken in front of the famous Pavilion, so all the nearby groups from Hove and Shoreham came down to bulk-up the photo. As it wouldn't involve campaigning Vicky allowed me to bring Jnr in the pram.

There were some familiar faces of people who had done the odd stint at Brexit corner but also, I got to meet some local councillors, specifically Anne Meadows (Labour) who was busy making sure she had everyone's email address. I spoke with her and we agreed to pool all email addresses afterwards. Also, Ian and I spoke with someone called Dee (?) who will crop up again later.

After the photo, we all made our way to Jury's Inn to a function room where there were speeches and some photographer from the Brighton Argus. I managed to catch a bit of it but Jnr started disrupting things so I just stood outside wrestling with him and trying to chat to people individually as they left. This meant I didn't get a chance to make a little speech in public which was a shame, worse still I never got to listen to who was who in the neighbouring groups, and worst of all I never got to tell Chris to give my regards to Dave!

Friday 6th May

Again, it's strange how the past can crop up. In the emails flying around one name caught my eye –

Stuart Scotland, I had worked with a project manager by that name back in 2008 on a project in Chelsea, could it be the same person? Sure enough it was! I seem to remember he had once given me a bollocking about something, but hey ho, I probably deserved it, and even if he had been in the wrong there were definitely no hard feelings on my part, he was right now, when it really mattered.

Saturday 7th May
Brexit corner – here I am with two councillors, I remember one was Labour and the other was Tory.

Monday 9th May
Published *'Has the EU Given us Peace?'* This was a fairly decent essay but it got very few hits (30) primarily because I didn't share it with any enthusiasm as it's subject matter was so depressing. I will (very reluctantly) outline the main points:

1, The Second World War ended in 1945. In 1957 six countries signed the Treaty of Rome, there are now twenty-eight countries in the EU. There are about fifty countries in Europe, yet the EU claims credit for *all* the peace enjoyed by *all* of Europe since 1945! So, they are claiming credit for events before the EU historically, and beyond the EU geographically.

2, What about the ethnic cleansing in the former Yugoslavia? Or the mass murders in Paris and Brussels? Do those deaths somehow not count? Are we not counting those sort of deaths today?

3, For decades, war between nation states has been in decline across the world, this is not a phenomenon exclusive to the EU. The EU (understandably) conflates nation states with war and union with peace, but in the modern world, wars tend to be fought for religion rather than national identity. Every country between Nigeria and China is involved in a military conflict. Why? Religion. Take the religious wars out of the equation and the world is more or less at peace.

"The horrible truth is that Europe is at war and the real fascists are winning – a genuinely extreme right-wing ideology that is homophobic, patriarchal, supremacist, creationist, militaristic, monocultural and authoritarian is advancing, yet even as increasing numbers of women, artists, journalists and intellectuals are bullied into silence the EU manically repeats it's claim that it has given us peace. They make a desert and call it peace."

Tuesday 10th May

After work, I got a bus to Kemp Town to deliver some leaflets to Brexit Vicki. On the quiet Vicki had been delivering leaflets to hundreds of homes whilst walking her dogs. It wasn't till too late that I realised delivering leaflets was actually one of the most effective ways of campaigning. This is why:

1, It gets your argument, how you want to present it directly into people's homes, so people have to pick them up and look at them just to throw them away. And even if they hate you they will pick it up and look at it just to work out exactly how much hate you deserve.

2, It bypasses the mainstream media which was run overwhelmingly by them, for them, against us.

3, In a whole day's campaigning at the street stall you may only hand out leaflets to fifty people and talk to say ten people for half an hour, whereas delivering leaflets allows you to get your message to 50 people every hour.

4, When someone picks up a leaflet they know that your campaign is active but they have no idea how active. The facelessness of this means that when you get a leaflet from the other side it's very demoralising because you imagine that millions of other houses have got the same leaflet when in reality it may only be a few dozen.

So, delivering leaflets is unglamorous slow and tiring, but it's how to win, and if I had to do it again, I would deliver more leaflets earlier. For this reason, it's entirely possible that without any fuss, whilst walking her dogs, Vicki won us more votes than all the rest of the Brighton Brexiteers put together! Significant things are made from mundane elements.

Vicki said she had been getting lots of her information from Guido Fawkes, I said I would check out his website. As usual I put on a brave face but

Vicki was the only person I met who was always certain of victory.

Thursday 12th May

On this day, Governor of the Bank of England Mark Carney issued a statement saying that the referendum on EU membership was *"the most immediate and significant risk for the UK's economic outlook"*.

I accept that in recent years the role of central bankers has become more politicised. It would be hard to imagine Carney's predecessor Mervyn King allowing the BoE to get dragged into a political fracas, and it would be inconceivable that King's predecessor *'Steady'* Eddy George would have inveighed in a highly-charged issue on behalf of The Bank, but this was of another order. The Governor of the Bank of England was actually tipping the markets to short it's own currency. Why? To create turbulence that could be blamed on the 'risk of Brexit'. The professional thing to do would have been to issue the most boring statement possible, reassuring the markets that we were prepared for any eventuality, but the establishment weren't interested in professionalism any more, just in maximising fear with a wall of pseudo-objective pro-EU propaganda.

How had the country's central bank become reduced to a political tool? Let's follow the money to find out: As governor, Mark Carney is paid £880,000 per annum, how did he get that job? He was appointed. By who? George Osborne, whose career depended on a remain vote. There's your answer. But I'm reluctant to criticise Carney, after all, if the Canadian government offered me £880,000 to whore out their central bank then I would probably do the same.

Also on this day *Brexit – The Movie* was released. When people had been talking about crowdfunding this project I couldn't really see the point of it, but on watching it I realised how important it was to do this. A movie was the perfect format to go through these issues as it could employ a large number of words and pictures for a full ninety minutes to walk the viewer through what were fairly complex arguments. The problem with Brexit the Movie however, was that it came to the subject very much from a free-market perspective, repeatedly making the point that freedom from the EU would mean freedom from bureaucratic regulations, when the point should have been that electing our own lawmakers might make us more right-wing, or more left-wing, but it would definitely make us more democratic, and that that was a good in itself. So, while Brexit the Movie was well made, it tended to sell independence to people that already believed in it.

Came across a great quote from philosopher Roger Scruton which I should have done more with:

"Building a political order without a reverse gear or without the ability to change in accordance with the needs of the moment is the greatest political mistake. It is the mistake of making a political order that won't recognise mistakes."

The interesting thing about this statement is that it identifies something that only became wholly apparent to me after the referendum – that Europe had essentially become a religion. Whereas reasonable people view evidence and question things

75

as they proceed, the EU's origins were so well intended, that to dissent had become heresy, hence the self-flagellation of the Euro and the manic accusations of thought crimes by their high priests.

Saturday 14th May

In 2012 David Cameron famously said that advocates of independence were *"fruitcakes, loonies and closet racists"* so on the way to Brexit corner I popped into the bakers and picked up some fruitcake to offer passers-by. I don't think it won us many votes.

I had an argument with someone who favoured the EU because they were against the House of Lords and the Monarchy. Certainly, I wouldn't go out of my way to defend either of those institutions, but it was odd how some people were affronted by unelected lords who could only amend law, and by a monarch who only had symbolic power, but cock-a-hoop for an unelected Commission that was assuming control of every aspect of our lives. I offered them some cake. They didn't want any.

Also, on this day, in a clear breach of ethical guidelines, adverts for Remain appeared on the politics page of the BBC's website. Websites don't run adverts for free, so there was only one possible explanation - money had been transferred from Remain to the national broadcaster.

Monday 16th May

Writing in the Guardian Paul Mason calls for Brexit – but just not yet! So now we could add his name to the list of 'left wing intellectuals' who bottled it along with Owen Jones, George Monbiot and Jeremy Corbyn. Even Noam Chomsky, Yanis

Varofakis and Slavoj Zizek had aired misgivings about Britain governing itself! I put it to you that these are the very people who spend their whole lives calling for a mass movement of collective action by ordinary working people against the neoliberal elite, but when the biggest mass movement of working people in British history took place right under their noses, it just wasn't trendy enough for them, the cause of self-government was somehow not worthy enough to merit their support, it was all just a bit too ... what's the phrase? ... working class! So, this would be another little titbit of advice for any would-be revolutionaries out there: Whatever you do, don't wait for the sophisticated left-wing intellectuals to lead you because when the hour comes they will indulge the very system that they profess to abhor. For the faint hearts, the ignominy of history awaits. But not everyone writing in the Guardian pissed their pants, John Harris, Larry Elliott and Giles Frazer can be very proud of their work.

Lets dwell on this for a second and take, for example, Yanis Varoufakis. Here is someone whose intelligence and integrity are beyond question, and with whom I am in near-complete agreement: He thinks it's virtually impossible to successfully reform the EU. So do I. He thinks Greek people should be able to change economic and social policies by voting for change. So do I. He says *"Brussels is a democracy-free zone"*. He is correct. But the second it comes proposing what should actually be *done* we part company, because I am a simple chap who reckons there's a simple change that would address these problems - its called independence - whereas he is a great intellectual who suddenly produces a dazzling

Burke-ian construct in which Greece can possess all the attributes of an independent democratic state without actually being one! A Schrodinger's EU in which everyone can simultaneously wave two flags forever! The fact that he is principled is beyond dispute, but with the best will in the world, he believes in a universe of square circles where establishment-conserving revolutionaries can spend their lives reforming the unreformable.

Tuesday 17th May
This was the date our daughter was due to be born. For weeks, I had known that the call could come at any time. My nerves were shredded.

Wednesday 18th May
Published *'Did Europe Give Britain Human Rights?'* Again, there's little point in re-rebutting every Remain falsehood here, if you actually *think* that *they* gave *us* the right to a fair trial, the right to privacy, freedom from torture, freedom from degrading treatment, freedom of religion, freedom of expression, freedom from discrimination, freedom from domestic violence and the abolition of slavery, then my debunking of that is already on the internet. Good work. 386 hits.

Friday 20th May
There was a plethora of anti-EU groups on Facebook and I would circulate essays and memes on their threads depending on the angle of the conversation. One such group was GBrexit (Guerrilla Brexit) set up by a guy called Jordan. It was getting traffic of about 500,000 views per week on Facebook and 20,000 on their website, and on this day Jordan

emailed to say that he had seen one of the essays I posted on his page and would I like to contribute some more?

GBrexit banged on about immigration a bit more than I would like but when you *have* to win you can't be picky about your bedfellows, and crucially GBrexit gave me the final piece of the jigsaw – a vehicle for the distribution of essays to a large number of people. I bit his hand off. One by one I passed my essays to him, he would then change the headline and the image to make it fit the style of his site and then he would publish it.

I don't know much about Jordan except that he is based in the North of England somewhere, but what I do know is that he was the Remain campaign's worst nightmare because he could do what I couldn't – make the issues comprehensible to large numbers of ordinary people - the readership he gave me dwarfed what I was getting on my blog or Facebook page.

Sat 21st May

At the stall today, Wayne brought some 'Lexit' leaflets (Left-wing Brexit) they were great, much better than the Vote Leave ones for campaigning in Brighton. There was a mobile number on the back, I texted:

"Hi, I run the Brighton Brexit group and we will need about 3,000 of your '#Lexit. The Left Leave Campaign' leaflets. Please let me know the ordering details Monday. Thanks S-"

Monday 23rd May

At work, I called the number on the back of the Lexit leaflet and spoke to someone called Rob

(Griffiths?) I said that as there was only a month left maybe he should just email me the artwork so I could print my own to save them time and money. I texted him my email address so we could sort it out straight away.

From my diary on this day: *'expose front organisations.'*

A trend was becoming apparent that many people campaigning for Remain were interested parties feigning impartiality. This is how it would work: The EU would identify opinion-forming groups in society: trade unionists, industrialists, charities, universities, research centres, arts organisations, environmental groups, credit rating agencies, farmers, human rights groups etc. etc. and then they would fund them.

They would pick a wide range of groups to fund but crucially they had to be authoritative and vocal. These organisations would then besiege the media masquerading as impartial experts and argue against independence whilst neglecting to mention their financial interest. It was a brilliant strategy, definitely the cleverest and most successful strategy of the entire campaign by either side. The EU was effectively employing an army of publicists, all with impressive titles and specialist knowledge (that was difficult for lay people to challenge) they were doing it with other people's money, and best of all, it was deniable.

For example, having signed the Kyoto Protocol the EU then failed to meet its targets and actually increased emissions. Primarily this was because EU law is drafted by a group of industrialists called the ERT. But did environmental groups speak out against this neoliberal monster? Of course not – The EU had bought them off!

Another example. The EU depressed workers' pay by insisting on the free movement of labour but then employed its stooges in trade unions to act as their de-facto spokesmen – campaigning against the interests of their own members!

Here's the best example: The EU would give grants to students. Nothing wrong with that I hear you say (and certainly it's a disgrace that the British Government no longer does) but the EU's motivation was not simply academic or altruistic. Naturally it's easier to spot the moral virtue in someone who gives you money, consequently every year another group of well-educated opinion-forming people would leave college feeling gratitude towards the EU for their education. Fair enough.

Lecturers in turn would see the EU grants coming into their colleges and would understandably be fearful that independence would mean fewer Euros, and because it's easier to spot the moral virtue in those that give you money, the lecturers would naturally advocate maintaining the system that maintained them. These lecturers, whose job it is to impart their greater knowledge to the students, also have the power to fail students so they are in positions of considerable influence, thus one pro-EU lecturer could influence successive intakes of students, and when they said: *'if it wasn't for the EU this or that person wouldn't be able to study here'* who could be so cold-hearted as to dissent?

So just by giving a small number of grants to a small number of students the EU managed to cultivate an entire ecosystem of pro-EU propaganda, or at the very least minimise the criticism the EU deserved for its ruination of Greece, Italy, Spain and Portugal. And it did this in universities – the very establishments that are traditionally hotbeds of anti-authority protest!

Now ask yourself, what system did Britain have before January 1973 when Heath signed us up to the EEC? Answer – colleges and students were properly funded by the national government, and all students received grants. Not loans. Grants. It was the golden age of British science and higher education. But while colleges today are acutely aware of the percentage of European funding they receive, they seem strangely forgetful of the much greater funding they received under the pre '73 system.

That was the beauty of the scam – whilst the money people received from the EU was tangible the vastly greater sums we contributed were not so:

1, Britain would give the EU a chunk of money.

2, They would keep about half.

3, They would distribute the other half back (to people who were oblivious to how much the EU took).

4, Those recipients would then campaign for everyone to carry on paying into the EU.

How on Earth did they lose? It was a brilliant, brilliant strategy – the EU had worked out how to bribe us with our own money, and as it continued it accumulated converts exponentially. Whichever EU official dreamt it up is undoubtedly a genius and should be put in charge of tackling climate change straight away!

Anyway, back to *'Expose front organisations'*, a pattern emerged:

1, Some member of the great and the good would pop up on the media extolling the virtues of EU membership.

2, I would then type their name into Wikipedia

3, Wikipedia would list their employers.

4, I would then go onto their employer's website and search for *'funding'* or *'annual report'*

5, I would then search the funding report for the word *'European'*

6, Lo and behold! They were receiving money from the EU!

Want some examples? Ok. We're talking about the IMF, the OECD, the IFS, the CBI, the TUC, the LSE, the NFU, the NUS, PwC, S&P, RSPB, WWF, FotE, the GMB, Unison etc etc…

This called for another essay straight away!

Tuesday 24th May

Daughter now a week overdue, exhausted with worry.

It was important with limited time and manpower not to leaflet the same streets twice so I set about making a master map. After work, I bought two A-Z books from the WH Smith shop in Brighton Station (I needed two because adjacent maps can be on both sides of the same page) I pulled all the pages out and stuck them together to make a big map showing every street. I then tried to work out from Brexit Vicki's emails where she had posted, and where the boundaries of Wish Ward were, which John Kapp had already done. But by the time I had got that far it was the early hours of the morning, I was exhausted and the map was hopelessly unwieldy. I folded it up, put it on top of my music stuff and forgot about it.

That was a huge mistake. It was a valuable resource that I should have passed on to Anne Meadows to help with the coordination of leafleting. It was another example of me exhausting myself financially and physically pursuing decent idea, but not taking it to the stage where it did any good.

Wednesday 25th May

On this day, I published *'Propaganda or Impartial Facts? How to Check'* in which I exposed the front organisations. Good Work. 413 hits.

Still no email from Rob at Labour Leave so I texted:

"Hi Rob, if you could just let me know who could email me the JPG/PDF then I could do the rest. Thanks S-"

He replied! *"Have PDF will forward later!"*

I replied, *"Ace also JPG would be handy too, thanks!"*

I got a message from Joe Hoover, referring me to an essay published on *'The Disorder of Things'* forum which he edits called *'The EU Referendum: Brexit, the Politics of Scale and State Transformation'*. I was a bit apprehensive about reading it as academic texts can be heavy going and also because I was scared it might be a morale-destroying debunking of everything I was fighting for. It got worse, the piece was written by Lee Jones who I remembered from a previous essay about sanctions called *'Societies Under Siege'* which I completely disagreed with, but I had a go and gave it a read. It was brilliant, electrifying; to this day the most devastating and authoritative case against the EU I've seen; and written completely from a genuinely progressive perspective. I just wish I had it to hand when Mike had posted the Yanis Varoufakis video on my time line!

I doubt Jones' essay will have won us many votes because although the second half was devastating, the beginning would have been hard going for most people; but it was good to know we now had an essay with which we could claim the intellectual high ground. I circulated it wherever I felt it could help.

Message from Jordan: *"the other article of yours I posted earlier got 6,000 hits so far ... But that does not take into consideration people who go to the website to share it. Most articles get between 5K and 25K views. Some of the more shared ones get 30K to 50K. It got 539 likes on the website so far which is awesome!"*

Thursday 26th May
"Hi Rob, I still don't have it. If you give me their number I'm happy to chase it so I don't need to keep pestering you. Ace! Seb."

That evening Ian popped round and picked up the street stall stuff. He was the boss now. Since the first Brexit corner I had said I might not be there for the next couple of weeks because the baby could turn up at any time. I had said this so often the rest just laughed when I repeated it, but this weekend it was the real deal, if there were no contractions by Sunday Vicky would be induced.

Friday 27th May
A nice guy I know who worked at the Guardian called Tim posted on Facebook about how Cameron was the worst Prime Minister in history for leading the country to this dangerous and unnecessary situation. In response I posted a link to my essay, *'Should Labour Back Brexit?'* His response had the cogency that only comes from spending years

working as an editor *"stop trolling my treads with your out-of-date propaganda"*. Ten words, succinct and brutal. Good writing. I squawked that I was the one who was campaigning to end Cameron's career and that he should be patting me on the back – but I had been stung and from that point on I never posted anything to a specific person, only to the Internet in general. He replied but I didn't read it.

Saturday 28th May
Brexit corner without me. I worried about them.

Sunday 29th May
A timetable for induction was agreed. We decamped to the Royal Sussex Hospital, Vicky's waters were broken that evening.

When writing an essay, it's important to have an angle so people can quickly grasp what it's about, but as we have seen it's difficult to write a general short, compelling essay against the EU because the subject is large geographically and historically, and because it's been deliberately designed to be incomprehensible; so, every essay had to be specific to be short. But then in the hospital it came to me! I could write a series of one line statements each contrasting the Remain/Leave position, that could summarise all the other arguments. Why hadn't I thought of it earlier? Hopefully I could get it written while it could still do some good. Vicky's contractions had just started. I frantically managed to draft the first two paragraphs on my phone before the contractions really got going.

Monday 30th May
Daughter born.

Tuesday 31st May
Busy doing other stuff.

Wednesday 1st June
Posted on Facebook. *"We have a lovely new daughter – Brexit Handley!"* The accolades rolled in.

Saturday 4th June
Baby duty, so no Brexit corner for me this day, but at least I knew it was in safe hands with Ian running it – or so I thought! The next day Paul informed me of a fracas involving a VIP! Apparently, our local MP Caroline Lucas (Green) had walked past the stall with a friend and noticed some of Paul's propaganda spread out for everyone's perusal. One item in particular, caught her eye – a laminated sign (not leaflet) quoting her.

There had been a brief and polite exchange of opinions, regarding the context of the quotation, and then Caroline and her friend departed. Then a few seconds later Paul noticed his sign had gone and joked about it with Wayne. But Wayne observed that because the sign wasn't one of the free leaflets, technically it shouldn't have been taken. There was no time to lose! With a cry of *"hey stop!"* our heroes gave chase and retrieved their item. No one was hurt. Twenty minutes later several Green Party activists turned up to have a nose around, but by then the offending article was safely packed away where it couldn't cause any more mischief.

Sunday 5th June

On this day former Prime Minister John Major appeared on the Andrew Marr Show where he described the leave campaign as: *"fundamentally dishonest and dishonest about the cost of Europe"*. He went on: *"I think their campaign is verging on the squalid … what they have done now … is to feed out to the British people a whole galaxy of inaccurate and frankly untrue information … They are a deceit … if they can't be straightforward and honest on a clear-cut matter of fact … upon what else can we trust them? … I am angry at the way the British people are being misled … I regard that as deceitful … this is a deceitful campaign"*

Ive gone through the transcript. There are 19 instances where he used words like *'dishonest'* or *'misled'* to allege that independence was being sold on a lie. But how many actual *facts* did he employ to support his argument? Well, 11 times he speculates that the future would be very bad if we declared independence; but because the future doesn't exist yet it contains no facts (except the laws of physics and algebra) therefore statements about the the future are not facts, but guesses. So I repeat, how many actual *facts* does he employ? Only one: *"We would face a tariff barrier of probably about 10%"*

1, The '*Common External Tariff*' varies on different goods but is generally below 10%

2, Tariffs can be renegotiated anytime without fuss, by mutual agreement.

3, Worldwide, the average tariff rate has declined steadily from about 20% in 1933 to 3% today - tariffs are dying out.

4, Tariffs only apply to goods and 40% of our EU trade is in services.

5, No trade on goods is without costs: We can either pay a membership fee and no tariffs or we pay tariffs and no membership fee. So obviously we are better off paying tariffs that are getting smaller all the time, rather than an EU membership fee that's getting bigger all the time.

6, Our trade with the EU is steadily declining from 30% in 1980 to 17% today.

The above is an example of how to argue using facts. Here's another example: In the same interview John Major said: *"We are outside the Eurozone, we are not responsible for their debts"*. This was incorrect because Britain does indeed contribute to the '*EU stabilisation mechanism*' that was used to prop up the Euro. Then to top things off Major claimed: *"I did negotiate the opt-out of the single currency"*. Well, I suppose that's one way of describing Black Wednesday! This is no corinthian elder-statesman - it's just a bloke who walked into a TV studio and started calling people names.

Monday 6th June
Writing in the Telegraph William Hague published an essay entitled '*The Leave campaign can't keep dodging the biggest question*' in which he had the

audacity to claim we hadn't provided details about how independence would work – as if external rule was transparent and functional! As if there was no subterfuge about what the EU leaders had in mind for their citizens! I never worked out whether William Hague was the most over-rated parliamentarian of the modern age or whether he had just agreed to be an outrider for every shit government idea. I don't know, but to be honest I haven't given it that much thought.

Tuesday 7th June.
Published *'Brexit – Your Questions Answered!'* This one was easy because I just listed all the main questions levelled by Hague and answered each one with exactly the same sentence: *"The policy would probably be quite similar to the policy we had in 1972, and if it were found that this arrangement wasn't working then we would VOTE to fix it."*
In your *face* William Hague! (402 hits)

Wednesday 8th June
In Brighton, a debate had been set up by the Argus paper. Dan Hannan, Rory Bloomfield, Caroline Lucas and Peter Kyle would be debating and answering questions. Vicky had given me a pass for the night so I went straight from putting Jnr to bed but still turned up late. The debate was pretty lousy. Hannan was decent but I already knew his arguments from YouTube. The arguments of Lucas and Kyle covered the whole spectrum from boring, right the way through to disingenuous.
Again, I never got to ask a question as I was right at the back, but generally it was sad how misinformed the audience were – and I'm referring

to both sides here – even among people who had bothered to attend the grasp of the basic issues was not great – the whole debate seemed dominated by tribal allegiances and emotional spasms rather than factual argument.

Paul, Ian and Brexit Vicki were there. Afterwards Vicki was fuming about the factual errors in Lucas' arguments but there was no time to chat – we positioned ourselves at the exits and handed out leaflets. I offered to explain things to anyone feeling confused. Afterwards I saw Dan Hannan standing outside chatting to someone. I was going to introduce myself but I had an urgent strategy meeting to attend with Ian and Paul at the World's End pub.

Here I need to talk about the polls, because by this point I was checking them non-stop.

Because Remain had been so successful in creating a social stigma about Brexit, people were reluctant to publicly admit they agreed with us, and this seemed borne out by the fact that we consistently did better in the anonymous internet polls than the telephone polls. Additionally, if I were to put a picture of the baby on Facebook it would get 'likes' and comments, but anything about Brexit would be completely ignored by everyone, and remember, here I was espousing a view that was held by about half the population. So many of my Facebook 'friends' seeing my pro-independence posts must have been sympathetic but simply internalised their approval rather than endure the condemnation that would have come from publicly agreeing. Now it's very frequent in elections for pollsters to underestimate support for the unfashionable party by about 4% but Brexit had become such an emotive issue it could easily have been about 6% in this instance. In addition to this I felt it would be much more likely that Remain supporters would abstain or fail to vote than our supporters. I felt this because among Remain there were people like Mason, Jones, Monbiot and Corbyn who whilst favouring EU membership harboured deep and genuine misgivings, whereas virtually no one favouring independence was plagued by existential doubts. For these reasons, even in the darkest moments when we seemed 6 to 7% adrift in the polls I knew there was hope. But having said all that something very odd had started happening – the polls had started moving our way! It had begun almost imperceptibly – from around mid-March the number of *'undecideds'* had begun to dwindle, the Remain support had stayed fairly constant at 43%, but apart from one dip in the second week of May our support had slowly crept up by about 1% every month until by early June the trend was so consistent it couldn't be denied any longer, we were on course to win!

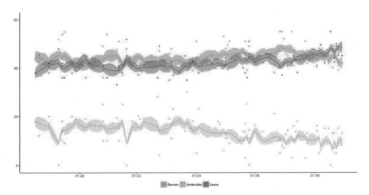

And as the days went by the realisation emerged that the Remain campaign simply wasn't winning any votes. Frantically Cameron, Brown, Kinnock,

Ashdown, Carney, Osborne, Major, Milliband, Clegg, Lagarde, Juncker and Obama pulled the same old political levers only to find that they weren't working anymore. They had tried all their ideas, thrown everything at us, spent vast sums of money and demonised us, but their poll ratings remained stubbornly horizontal. They simply couldn't offer us anything safer, more desirable or less expensive than self-rule, so the only option left was to just ramp up the fear, and the more those millionaire masters of the universe shrieked at us not to change anything the more hysterical their arguments appeared. I remember thinking to myself *"this is the week Remain lost it – a couple more days of this and their campaign will implode altogether."* At last it was their turn to look into the abyss.

Anyway, back to the drink with Ian and Paul at the World's End pub. We discussed the polls and Paul observed that the more factual information we got out the more our support grew and so the key was to just keep pumping out as much factual information as possible to as many people as possible. I think he was absolutely right in this, but whether you agree or not you can bet your life in Remain HQ they will have been saying precisely the opposite.

I can't remember much else about that night but I do remember Paul saying that the day after William Hague said there would not be a referendum on the Lisbon Treaty *"because there's no longer anything to have a vote about"* he cancelled his Tory party membership. That's why you have to rate Paul – he acted on principle, and it's because not enough others do the same we find ourselves governed by people like William *'Genius Statesman'* Hague rather

93

than Paul *'Gets It'* Perrin. But let's just imagine for a minute that Hague had said the opposite and called *for* a referendum. Then Britain would have probably rejected the Lisbon Treaty and would today find itself in a slightly reformed EU. So maybe Hague really *is* a genius statesman who postponed the democratic reckoning so that when it inevitably came it swept away more of the rot! ... Or then again, maybe he isn't and he just got every big call wrong. Dunno.

Thursday 9th June

On this day, I received a council tax bill from Canterbury Council. Canterbury Council's apparently never ending campaign to smash my life could be a whole book in itself (not that I could ever bring myself to write it) but basically they had decided to address someone else's council tax bill to me for a flat that did not exist in a property I had never lived in, which I had bought in 2008 as a retirement home for my dad, but which I sold in 2013 (at a loss of £92,000) because my father (who was struggling with mental problems at the time) had set it on fire, smashed it to pieces and started forging my signature on various documents. Got that? Ok, well although everything had been explained to them two years earlier Canterbury Council decided June 2016 was a terrific time to start threatening me with court action for the money.

I called the help desk, they refused to accept any of my points, and said I needed to take up my appeal with the valuations office, I kept arguing with them, I said they were trying to destroy me, they hung up the phone on me, I felt as if I was having some type of breakdown, I kicked the safety gate at the top of the stairs, Vicky asked what I was doing, I told her to shut up. I said it twice. She said that was unacceptable. It was worse than that but I can't say here. I just had to hold my life together for another two weeks.

Friday 10th June
Phoned various valuations offices in South East England, couldn't get through to anyone. Bought a new child safety gate for the stairs.

Saturday 11th June
With relatives visiting the baby I was able to sneak out to Brexit corner. At last we had some decent leaflets entitled *'The Choice'* which were the best ones Vote Leave produced. I would hold them up and proclaim, *"should we stay or should we go?"* And then improvise depending on what people shouted back. That day England were playing Russia at Euro 16 in France. Every person wearing a football shirt who walked past gladly took a leaflet.

Sunday 12th June

A brief aside about comments and replays.

Comments on my time line. Generally, I didn't post arguments to specific people unless I was replying to them, and since incurring Tim's wrath I had stopped altogether, but more and more stuff was being directed at me personally. Two people in particular were posting Remain arguments on my time line on an almost daily basis which started to feel like an attack. Initially I rejoined, but as the vote got closer responding increasingly became a waste of energy.

Comments on my blog. Whenever I got a comment on my blog, WordPress would ask me if I wanted to edit/approve it. I prided myself on always approving and never editing. Often the arguments would appear impressive on first scan but once answered the authors would default to bluster. They are there for all to see.

Comments on my Declare Independence page. Because I believe in free speech I am loath to delete any comments or block trolls and generally I kept to this rule. Besides, crap arguments posted on my page were actually welcome because they allowed me and the other page users to publicly knock them down. The ultimate compliment I could pay anyone would be to block them as that would be an admission that their arguments could lose us votes, and I did block a few people, but only at the end when it would have just taken too much time and effort to explain why they were wrong.

So, at the beginning it was about winning the argument, whereas towards the end it was just about winning the vote.

Monday 13th June
"Brexit could be the beginning of the destruction of not only the EU but also Western political civilisation, in its entirety." Donald Tusk, European Council President.

Here we have the classic Remain argument:

1, It's conservative – he is arguing against change.

2, It's designed to spread fear.

3, It's an emotional spasm rather than a reasoned argument.

4, It conflates the EU with peace.

5, It conflates the EU with civilisation.

6, It contains no empirical facts.

7, It speculates about the future, and because the future doesn't exist yet this means it's unfalsifiable.

8, The person saying it has money and prestige.

9, The person saying it receives money from the European Union.

Ok. I've just referred to *'falsification'* and I hate jargon so if you haven't got time to swot up on Karl Popper, I'll quickly explain what I mean. Here are the various Remain arguments, see if you can spot what they all have in common:

1, Vote Remain or you are racist.

2, Vote Remain or you are inward-looking.

3, Europe has given us peace.

4, If we declare independence you will lose your job.

5, If we declare independence there will be a recession.

6, Vote Remain or Boris Johnson will be Prime Minister.

Spot it? No fact can invalidate any of these statements, but virtually any fact could be somehow claimed to validate them. But being unfalsifiable doesn't mean these statements are facts, it means they are opinions – their unfalsifiability is their weakness not their strength. They are not part of a rational argument but a belief system.

Throughout this story, I assert that it was actually the advocates of independence who were the real progressives, and that Remain were the real far-right conservatives, but obviously Remain would say the same about me, so how does the reader chose between us? I think the difference is that I try to justify my position with examples that are falsifiable which any bod can check for themselves on Wikipedia. For example, if independent democracies tended to have high unemployment, low growth, no children, authoritarian tendencies and dysfunctional government then my argument would be falsified and I would have to concede I was wrong. But they don't, and Eurozone countries do.

Conversely, imagine you are in the Remain camp and you have to sell the EU to people; an EU that has frozen the GDP of member states, and generated unemployment on an industrial scale, an EU where people have simply stopped having children, an EU that won't even discuss the Islamic war, an EU that is a plutocracy which has frozen pay and which is increasing pollution and inequality. How do you sell that shit? With facts? Of course not! The only card they had was an appeal to an emotional spasm, to tribalism; an appeal not to *actual* progressivism but the *idea* of progressivism; to make people scared or to somehow make it a referendum on the character of Johnson or Farage. And how do you conceal that your campaign is fact-free hysteria? By making exactly that claim about your opponents: because we wanted to elect our lawmakers, somehow it was *us* who were the *'far right'*. And how do I prove that I'm not a racist? Well obviously, I can't. Just like their predictions of a post-Brexit recession, their accusations of bigotry were unfalsifiable. So, Remain arguments tended to be either guesses about the future, opinions about people or appeals to our nature (unfalsifiable) whereas our arguments tended to be comparisons or observations (falsifiable). The whole thing was pretty much a straight re-run of Karl Popper's argument with the Frankfurt School – with Donald Tusk and his cohorts denying the reality of the EU because they loved the *idea* of it; and employing pseudoscience, opinion and technical jargon to conceal their shortcomings.

Later that day Paul visited with some Green Leaves posters, which were the first hand-outs we had that really challenged people. They were A4 size – the front was a window poster and the back had more detailed information. But the thing that was really different about them was that they directly countered what I called the *'bedfellows'* argument.

The bedfellows argument consisted of *'cool people agree with me whereas uncool people agree with you'*. The first problem with the bedfellows argument is that, well, it's not actually an argument – just a way of reducing the conversation into a popularity contest between the prominent protagonists. But the bigger problem with the bedfellows argument was that it worked, because the vast geo-political pros and cons of Brexit/Bremain were so complex, arguing about people's bedfellows often sufficed for debate.

Admittedly the bedfellows argument was used by both sides throughout the campaign, and I suppose my cry of *'Brex-Terminate Cameron'* made me guilty of it too, but Remain used it more for two reasons:

1, Their other arguments weren't very good either.
2, More uncool people really did agree with us.

Personally, I would have been happy to talk about the issues (rather than the personalities) all day long, but time and again we were getting hit with the bedfellows argument: *"but Johnson is a clown"* ... *"but Farage is a bigot"* (as if it was a referendum on them!) We were being called Nazis, Racists, Fascists, Flat-Earthers and knuckle-draggers, and we had to have an answer for that or we would have lost, and the Green Leaves posters were the first ones to totally confront this. When you're standing in a street handing out anti-EU leaflets printed by the Green Party and they have Tony Benn on the front then however tribal people's allegiances are, they *have* to think twice - it was an information bomb.

Tuesday 14th June

Paternity leave over, back to work, and after weeks pestering them I actually got a delivery of 2,000 Labour Leave leaflets – but they weren't the leaflets I had asked for – no wonder those guys never win anything!

I contacted Green Leaves and ordered a few thousand Tony Benn posters.

Vote Leave had sent a *'Top Secret'* strategy document outlining what to do for the rest of the campaign. I scanned it. Their general strategy seemed to be that we should try to make the campaign more boring, less emotive and take some heat out of the rhetoric, lull the Remainers into a false sense of security and organise our core support to make sure they got to the polling station. I can appreciate what they were trying to do but reading it just clarified that we had to work primarily on our own initiative. It could no longer be orchestrated, they could wave their batons as much as they liked, but every player was improvising.

From my diary: *'email office re Brexit'*. Thankfully I didn't. On one day, I wore my Brexit t-shirt under my shirt, with the intention of walking round without my shirt in the afternoon, but I felt a bit sheepish about it so I didn't. Wise move.

Donated £10 to Vote Leave

Wednesday 15th June

Received another 5,000 of the wrong leaflets from Labour Leave, maybe they had mixed up my order, but they weren't that bad, and over the next few days I brought the boxes home.

Published a short essay called *'What is British Music?'* In it I wondered whether the British psyche is somehow generated by our geography? That when we regard Britain on a world map it becomes evident that we must be apart and distinct and that this is why the music that resonates most with British people is the music of the outsider. And I don't just mean the obvious examples like Morrisey, Lennon, Lydon, Bush, Bowie, Barrett, Drake, McColl, Innes or Formby, but going right back to Elgar and Blake. They were all oddballs, rejects and outsiders. But this essay was just a bit of light relief, and while I was onto something the argument needed more thought so I never bothered to circulate it.

On this day *Lexit the Movie* was released. Made in two weeks for £6,000 and apparently edited with a pair of scissors, it was car crash movie making.

Personally, I love the charm of all things amateur, but *Lexit the Movie* was so cobbled-together, it was arduous to watch. However, having said that, in terms of raw content it contained more challenging arguments than the more professional *Brexit the Movie*. George Galloway was featured throughout. As an admirer of Christopher Hitchens, I admit it felt uncomfortable to find myself on the same side as Galloway, but again, when you *have* to win you can't be picky about your bedfellows.

Lexit the Movie was made by Labour Leave who had really pissed me off by taking ages to send me the wrong leaflets, but clearly Labour Leave were just like the rest of us – a bunch of guys who meant well, who had taken on a lot of work and who were struggling to keep on top of it all. The tragedy though was that Labour Leave were so perfectly placed to influence the result. If their film was better put together and had come out two months earlier it would have won us tens of thousands more votes.

This was also the day of the infamous Thames Flotilla debacle. As if things weren't ridiculous enough already Admiral Farage had decided to lead a flotilla of pro-Brexit fishermen up the Thames only to be intercepted by a rival fleet lead by First Sea Lord Bob Geldof replete with sound system playing *'I'm In with The In Crowd'*. One day someone is going to write an opera about this shit.

Someone called David called round to pick up some leaflets. By now our little house had become Rebel Warehouse Central with boxes of leaflets everywhere. Almost every day someone else would turn up, we would smile, shake hands, load up a box or two and I would wish them well. This Wednesday was the last of a handful of halcyon days when the future seemed bright and hopeful. We were doing good work, confidence was surging, Remain were imploding, the polls were going our way, and every Remain argument could be breezily dismissed as the manic ravings of sore losers.

Thursday 16th June

Green Leave leaflets arrive. Green Leave were a serious outfit. Remain were bloody lucky that Labour Leave weren't as well organised as Green Leave!

At the office, some of the associates had *'IN'* posters on their desks. I kept my mouth shut.

That lunch time I took some leaflets to Exmouth Market and handed them out. I handed out the Green Leave Tony Benn posters, the Labour Leave booklets and some booklets about TTIP which surprisingly, a few people were actually interested in! Nick and Peter, two of the company directors walked past. Nick gave me a sly smile over his glasses. He probably thought I was just a bit of a nutter, but keeping my ranting out of his office turned out to be a very good call as British politics was about to spiral out of control in the most horrifying way imaginable. News reports were emerging that a female Labour

MP had been attacked. Amid the hustle and bustle of campaigning I didn't follow the story that closely.

Friday 17th June
It wasn't just an attack, she had been murdered. Her name was Jo Cox (Remain) and the police were holding someone called Thomas Mair who had been charged with murder. A quick image search on Google and there he was giving a Nazi salute.

Obviously, we all agree that this was an appalling act, and extend our sincere and deepest condolences to the family and friends of the victim; and we all hope the murderer receives the severest possible punishment. Of course, I feel that way and I'm sure you do too, but politics is a cynical art, so, accepting all that how did this tragedy play out politically? Well if someone ever does write Brexit The Opera and they portray Cox and Mair accurately, then critics would accuse them of making up caricatures because Jo Cox was as close to an angel as one could imagine whereas Thomas Mair was pretty much the living embodiment of an action movie villain.

She was a completely decent, likeable mother of two young children, pretty and petite (about 5'). She had become an MP after years of charity work and was especially concerned about refugees. He was an unemployed, angry white middle-aged loner who dressed in military fatigues and who had purchased Neo-Nazi literature online. She had spent the morning visiting a local charity in her West Yorkshire constituency and was on her way to hold her surgery when he had stabbed and shot her multiple times shouting *"Britain First!"* He didn't just attack a lady, he killed a wonderful lady who was probably about a foot shorter than him. With weapons. And his motivation was hate. Momentarily I wondered whether it was all just some incredibly sick hoax. It was impossible to comprehend without revulsion.

Ok, so imagine you are campaigning for Remain. You've spent all your money and its failed, you've pumped out every scare story you can think of and its failed, you've spent £9,500,000 sending everyone a propaganda booklet and its failed, you've had endorsements from everyone up to Obama and even that has failed, you're about to lose the most important vote in over 40 years, you're staring defeat in the face, your campaign is disintegrating ... and you get a gift like that? It was the political open goal of the century.

Did Remain seek to politicise Cox' death? Obviously, they would deny it, but obviously they did, and if you think they didn't, you are naive. Can I blame them for doing it? No, for two reasons:

1, If there been a disgusting act of Islamic terrorism on the same day, I'm sure some idiots on the Leave side would have tried to capitalise on it in a similar way.

2, Usurping external news events as vehicles for your political message is what political strategists do. It's their job.

Bottom line. Remain milked the killing of Joe Cox for everything they could. I'm not blaming them for doing it, I'm just saying, don't think they didn't because they did. Remain knew full well that from the jaws of defeat Thomas Mair had just handed them a *get out of jail free'* card, gift-wrapped, on a plate.

From that point onwards, Jo Cox was everywhere and the eulogies were never-ending, she replaced Cameron as their figurehead and we were the Mairites. After all our work, Thomas Mair had popped up from out of the blue, and in a few seconds of insanity appeared to confirm every stereotype about us and them. Appearing in court that day Mair claimed he had changed his name and now wanted to be known as, *'Death To Traitors.'* Classy. Maybe they call him *'Death'* for short.

Vote Leave emailed to say their campaign was suspended until further notice.

Vicky started getting in quotes for the new roof, in anticipation of getting her husband back in a week's time. I looked at the growing mould on the ceiling and thought about the money I had spunked on Brexit t-shirts I had given to homeless people.

Saturday 18th June

On this day there was an actual official strategy meeting at Hove Museum. Those in attendance:

Sir Andrew Bowden (former Conservative MP)
Anne Meadows (Labour councillor)
Tom Waterhouse (Labour councillor)
Ian Crawford (Brighton Brexiteers)
Sebastian Handley (Brighton Brexiteers)
Jnr Handley (Mascot)

Tom went through his agenda, but the killing of Joe Cox hung over everything and the latest opinion polls had showed an ominous reversal.

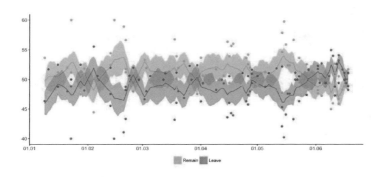

He had been in contact with Remain who insisted that as a mark of respect both sides suspend all campaigning till Monday, although low level canvassing like delivering leaflets was ok from Sunday afternoon onwards. Remain had said that if any of our team were seen campaigning they would take it to the press that we were callously indifferent to the tragedy. But the thing was, the rolling coverage of grieving for Jo Cox *was* a de facto campaign so essentially our operation was suspended whilst theirs was cranked up to number eleven with Jo Cox' greatest hits on repeat play.

Tom mentioned something about Paul Perrin. I said *"Oh, you know Paul?"* He shuffled uncomfortably. I hadn't checked my email for a while but evidently when Tom sent round a message about suspending the campaigning. Paul went ballistic and cc'd his reply to everyone else. Lots of us were cracking under the pressure.

Brighton and Hove were supposed to have two base camps over the last two days that would function as operations rooms from which Anne would direct leaflet distribution and volunteers would phone everyone on the telephone list. Again,

Tom shuffled uncomfortably, John Kapp had offered the use of his house but it was no longer possible to take up his offer.

"Why's that Tom?"

"He's just been arrested for criminal damage – the police apprehended him this week going along the A23 painting 'Vote Leave' on all the road signs"

I love John Kapp.

Anyway, everyone umm-ed and ahh-ed for a while till Ian said, *"How about just having one house then?"* and everyone agreed that was a good idea. Not the sort of guy to order a salad.

Apparently, Sir Andrew had given a speech in Kemp Town that week which had been well received, but Tom noted *"I'm not making a party-political point here Sir Andrew but several people were rather put out by your claim that what happened to Jo Cox was an 'occupational hazard'"*.

Caroline Penn
@ThePennyDrops

To the former MP who at UKIP hustings described what happened to Jo Cox as an "occupational hazard" - you are lower then vermin.

16 Jun 2016, 8:50 pm

40 RETWEETS   **37** LIKES

 Tommy Not Thomas @Tommy… 16 Jun
@ThePennyDrops you've got to be KIDDING me! That is truly atrocious!

   1

 kelvin newman @kelvinnewman 16 Jun
@ThePennyDrops for real?

   1

 Tommy Not Thomas @Tommy… 16 Jun
@ThePennyDrops Who? Where? When?
#NameAndShame

↩ ⇄ ♡

 Caroline Penn @ThePennyDrops 16 Jun
@TommyCoyneBN1 Sir Andrew Bowden,
KT.

↩ ⇄ 3   ♥ 1

 Tommy Not Thomas @Tommy… 16 Jun
@ThePennyDrops wait a minute.
Hustings suggests campaigning. Weren't
all such things suspended as a mark of
respect?

↩ ⇄ 1   ♡

 Caroline Penn @ThePennyDrops 16 Jun
@TommyCoyneBN1 Yep. That was
agreed, sadly organisers had other ideas.

↩ ⇄ 1   ♥ 1

GMB Sussex Branch @GMBS... 16 Jun
@ThePennyDrops out rages

↩ ⇄ ♥ 1

Tommy Not Thomas @Tommy... 16 Jun
@ThePennyDrops words fail me

↩ ⇄ ♥ 1

Jason Mark Ryder @JasonRy... 16 Jun
@ThePennyDrops all too predictable

↩ ⇄ ♥

Thomas Evans @ThomasEva... 17 Jun
@ThePennyDrops @TommyCoyneBN1
He's not a UKIP member is he?

↩ ⇄ ♥

(See the way they are campaigning whilst simultaneously *not* campaigning as a mark of respect?)

Sir Andrew explained to us that he had been on the IRA hit list back when they had blown up the Grand Hotel and killed Mountbatten. The police had advised him that the threat to his life was credible and that he should stop his constituency surgeries, but he refused because he believed that democracy must continue whatever the personal risks.

Comments that Sir Andrew was *'lower than vermin'* should be seen in this context.

I was trying to keep Jnr under control so I just suggested that they give me something very simple to do where I wouldn't be doubling up on anyone else's work. I had booked Wednesday and Thursday off work so we agreed I would just leaflet the main entrance to Brighton Station from 6am to 6pm both days, but that as I would need to put Jnr to bed at 6 we would need someone else to do 6-8. That was all agreed.

Sir Andrew asked if Tom or Anne had a Vote Leave Rosette he could wear at the count. Tom said he didn't but that because the design of the rosette was red he could lend Sir Andrew the Labour Party rosette that was in his van with a Vote Leave badge pinned to the front? Sir Andrew thought this was a splendid idea and Tom duly got the rosette from his van. Tom mused *"is this some sort of bucket list thing Sir Andrew, that for one day in your life you are going to wear a Labour rosette?"* Sir Andrew explained that normally it would be beyond the pale but that under the circumstances he was prepared to make an exception.

I had to get Jnr back for his nap and lunch, but on the way, I couldn't resist swinging by Brexit corner to see if anyone was there. Sure, enough Paul and Wayne were pumping the information. I didn't say they should stop, I wasn't their leader, Brighton Brexiteers didn't have any leaders, I just told them what had been said at the meeting. Once again Paul's response stuck in my mind *"I'm not campaigning, I don't know how to campaign, I'm just handing out information."* It was hard to tear myself away but I needed to get Jnr home. We shook hands and I wished them well. In my heart that boring, chewing gum stained bit of pavement will forever be Brexit Corner.

Sunday 19th June
Brexit Vicki came around to pick up some boxes of Labour Leave and Green Leave leaflets. I was under a cloud because I felt Thomas Mair had just lost it for us, but obviously, I hid my despondency from her. As usual I didn't ask whether she thought we would win, but when I mentioned the killing of Jo Cox Vicki looked me right in the eye, smiled and said: "*I'm still mega confident*"

But how did she gauge this? Opinion polls said we were losing, pro-Brexit posts on Facebook never got shared, virtually no one had a Vote Leave poster in their window so, presuming it wasn't bluster, what made her '*mega confident*'? Well it seemed she gleaned this from the many conversations she had with people who all conceded (virtually without exception) that they just could not defend the EU.

Here we come to a central philosophical argument of the campaign: the British operate in the mindset of empiricists like Locke or Hume whilst the 'continentals' operate more in terms of abstract truth a la Descartes or Kant. So, whilst we could all agree that the EU was based on laudable ideals the bottom line for the people Vicki was talking to was that it simply wasn't functional. The whole world could see it wasn't working, but while the intellectuals presented their denial as idealism, your average Brit saw the idealism as the problem not the solution. So how come Vicki called it right when no one else did? Well, to answer my own question, her conclusions were based on observable reality.

Nick, my best friend (and best man at my wedding) was visiting Brighton with his family.

His son saw the poster in the window and asked him *"Dad, are we remain or leave?"*

NT: *"We're Remain"*

I laughed and reassured Nick's son: *"We will still be friends"*.

Published *'Referendum – the Last Post. Phew!'* Good information. It got 229 views on my site but on the GBrexit page it got 188 shares!

Monday 20th June

In the Commons, MPs were meeting in a special session to pay tribute to Jo Cox, some speeches were touching and eloquent, others were dog whistle propaganda for the EU masquerading as compassion.

"Jo Cox didn't just believe in loving her neighbour... she saw a world of neighbours" Jeremy Corbyn.

Many MPs focused in on her claim that the different ethnic groups in her constituency had *'more in common'* than divided them. A laudable sentiment, but why do you think, out of all the good things Cox ever said, it was the phrase *'more in common'* that got put on repeat play?

Stephen Kinnock commented on the political context of the killing, which came hours after Nigel Farage had unveiled the *'breaking point'* poster:

"I can only imagine Jo's reaction had she seen the poster unveiled hours before her death...she would have responded with outrage and a robust rejection of the calculated narrative of cynicism, division and despair that it represents. Jo understood that rhetoric has consequences."

Clever one this. See how rather than share a memory of her he is talking about an event that never actually happened? And see how, rather than quoting her he is speculating about what he thinks she *might* have said? When is a eulogy not a eulogy? When it is delivered by someone whose parents have received more than £10,000,000 in pay, allowances, and pension entitlements from the EU.

Did the media speak about her excellent work concerning feminism and women's rights? To an extent, but mostly it was all about how we should *'come together'* to achieve what? *'Unity?'* Against what? *'Evil division!'*

This lunch time I did more leafleting at Exmouth Market. At one point someone said to me: *"Your side murder anyone who disagrees with them"*. That ended up being the number one insult I received through the whole campaign.

Also at the market that lunchtime, were about six remain people there with their *'IN'* bags. Whenever I saw one of those bags my heart would sink. That was our biggest failure, we were offering self-rule, the most noble thing in the world, whilst they were just offering neoliberal authoritarianism but somehow, they managed to make their cause cool, while we never did.

Tuesday 21st June
David Beckham comes out for Remain. No surprise that a millionaire at the pinnacle of society should be against changing anything.

Wednesday 22nd June
I had booked the Wednesday and Thursday off work, but got up earlier than usual, around 5:30. I got a load of the Green Leaves Tony Benn posters and the Labour Leave leaflets and brought them up to the

station. The Tony Benn posters had to go out now or never because no poster in a window would change anything after today. I was there at 6am. Nothing is more disheartening than campaigning on your own. Whenever I stood at the side entrance it looked like more people were coming in the front, and whenever I stood at the front entrance it looked like more people were coming in the side. Still I managed to get a fair amount of information out.

Dee walked past, I can't remember her full name but it began with D, she was from somewhere in Eastern Europe and I remembered her from the time Chris Grayling gave his speech in Brighton. Quite independently from me she had turned up with some of her own leaflets that she had printed herself. We only spoke briefly because there was campaigning to do. I said I was doing the front entrance so she did the side entrance, she said she could only stay for a while. I never saw her again. Maybe she didn't contribute much, maybe she did lots of campaigning that I wasn't aware of, but the point is she exactly fitted the Brexit profile: she was yet another person who did things for herself by herself, a self-motivating autonomous one-person campaign who didn't wait around for leaders. Just like me, Vicki, John Kapp and Paul Perrin and all the others she was a microcosm of the entire geo-political argument: on their side, there was a centrally organised monolithic structure handing down edicts to supine groups, whilst on our side there were independent people in independent groups campaigning for – independence. Both sides were the embodiments of the systems they advocated.

So anyway, there I was handing out leaflets outside the main entrance, putting on a brave face and feeling a bit sorry for myself when at about 7:30 the first of the Remainers turned up and said to me:

"You're not allowed to campaign there, and if you stay you will be told to move"

"Ok so when they ask me to move I'll move"

Now I had a huge grin on my face, he was the spineless living embodiment of his own philosophy, trying to instil fear, as if I should quail at the prospect of some technical sub-clause being implemented. I campaigned with full vigour until the morning rush was over then grabbed breakfast. I checked my email, Vote Leave had put the word out to not campaign at the stations for fear it might *'incentivise'* the opposition. I thought *'fuck that'* and carried on, I wasn't giving out their leaflets anyway.

Meanwhile mass rallies were being held to celebrate the life of Jo Cox, but the timing of this was not as cynical as might first appear – the 22nd of June would have been her 42nd birthday. Having said that it wasn't exactly a quiet family affair. There was a *'More in Common'* rally in Trafalgar Square, a minute's silence was held at Glastonbury and a vigil was held at the French National Assembly. Organisers said the events were to *"show the world we have more in common than that which divides us."*

President Obama got in on the act too: "Today people ... are *coming together* to honour the remarkable life of Jo Cox ... She believed in an idea that *transcends borders and cultures"* (my italics)

The BBC reported one speaker telling a crowd in Batley to *'unite against hate and division'*. A friend was reported as saying "Jo was ... A force for good, *bringing people together"* (my italics). Another friend was quoted as saying "I think there's something that she's touched in people's hearts that goes well *beyond Britain."* (my italics)

Let's presume that all this was not the mawkish usurpation of a private tragedy, how come the same wasn't done for Lee Rigby or Palmira Silva? Do their deaths somehow not count? I have not written one bad word about Jo Cox, but the establishment really could not have done any more to exploit the tragedy for their own ends. To quote a clever politician, it was a *'calculated narrative of cynicism'*.

Back at the station a few people called me *'fascist'* *'murderer'* and *'nazi'*, I just shouted back *"I love you!"* but I did have a couple of interesting conversations, one guy with a pink jumper was rude to me at first saying that I believed in a fantasy, I stammered that I just wanted to revert to a political system that worked pretty well up to 1973. Then a guy with a beard came up and called me a racist. To his credit the guy in the pink jumper took umbrage with this and showed himself to be the sort of thoughtful reasoned person of whom there were too few in the campaign, saying to beard guy something like:

"I believe in the EU but there are problems with how it works, it genuinely does need reform and if we just accuse people who disagree with us of being racist then we're not making proper arguments and were unlikely to reform anything."

I joked with him *"Don't forget to vote on Friday!"* He laughed and we shook hands.

By this time I had been asked to stand outside the boundary of the station by a friendly chap, which of course I was happy to do. As I carried my box of leaflets away the nearby stall holders cheered that I was leaving.

Got text from Brexit Vicki asking what was a good time to come to the station. I replied that it was now a bit quiet at the station and she would probably be better off doing the shopping centre, but extra help at the station would be good around 6pm. She replied:

"thanks for getting back to me but having spoken to Anne a little while ago apparently, the stations are now not to be targeted! You should have an email about it waiting for you so I have decided to pick up the election leaflet packs from Ian and start to do roads in Whitehawk this afternoon and then they are going to decide the plan for tomorrow and let us know – all very frustrating!! Vicki"

You see? There *was* no team, there *was* no plan, just lots of autonomous one-person campaigns.

I heard a horn bib, a cabbie driving into the taxi rank beckoned me over and asked for some literature, I had some car stickers too so I gave him a couple, then I heard another bib bib! And another … Why hadn't I thought of this earlier? The cabbies were ordinary workers, our natural supporters, they were centrally located and drove all around town. I gave all the rest of my car stickers to one guy who promised to distribute them to the other drivers. That was a good bit of campaigning, hopefully it wasn't too late. The lesson here is you can't have a nice surprise without varying how you do stuff.

Around midday it was a bit quiet and I wasn't getting many leaflets out. So, I checked with Anne whether the houses to the west of the station had been done. She said they hadn't so I dragged my stuff up the hill and did a few streets. Handy tip – you can get more leaflets to more people if you target the streets where the houses don't have long garden paths. That's why I did these streets, because the front doors were right at the pavement I could get double the leaflets out in the time I had. My box split, I scrambled round on the pavement to pick up all the leaflets. Then back to the station to catch the commuters.

Around nine Green Party people campaigning for Remain turned up and surrounded me, they took issue with the fact that some of my leaflets were the Green Leave leaflets featuring Tony Benn. One very irate lady came right up to my face:

"Just give me a one word answer, do you really think if Tony Benn were alive today he would be campaigning with Nigel Farage, yes or no?"

"Yes"

"You're mad"

Well she had asked for a one word answer. But fortunately, she came back to tell me more about how mad I was, which allowed me to explain that in 1975 Tony Benn campaigned with Enoch Powell who was an infinitely more frightening prospect than Nigel Farage and that Benn was more concerned with democratic control over the powerful than hanging out with the trendies.

Reinforcements turned up! Wayne arrived and stood with me. He had with him the latest edition of Socialist Worker with its huge 'VOTE LEAVE' headline. We stuck it on the front of our leaflet box. Time and again I held out leaflets to people declaring: *"There is hope!"*

By six it was time for me to go back to put Jnr to bed. I hated to leave Wayne there to campaign on his own with all those pesky Remainiacs trying to drown him out, but I had promised Vicky I would do bath time. I left my bag with him and he said he would drop it off round mine once he was done. A couple of hours later he called round with the bag. I asked if he had had any trouble with the Remain crowd, he replied: *"often outnumbered, never out-gunned!"*

That night I stayed up till about 1AM putting a blog together listing *'The Best of Brexit!'* articles and videos. With them all set out in one essay it meant I would only have to send one link to people who wanted clear information. I wished I had thought of it earlier, but maybe it got us a couple of votes.

Thursday 23rd June

I got up at 5:45 for the *'dawn raid'* to deliver leaflets to some place called Moulscombe, apparently it was Anne Meadow's ward. Vicky had barely slept and I kept apologising that I had to leave.

I texted Ian, did I need to bring any leaflets? He replied *"no"*. Not the sort of guy to order a salad.

I went downstairs and the kitchen was flooded, the rain had been dripping through the ceiling all night and the bucket to catch it was overflowing. I quickly cleaned it up. Vicky said the roof had to be fixed soon because Jnr could slip on the tiles. There was a large mouldy damp patch on the ceiling, the babies were crying, I kept apologising. I promised I would sort it the very next day.

Words from Dylan's *'the Ballad of Hollis Brown'* sprang to mind. *"Your wife's screams are stabbing you like the dirty driving rain"*. No one was screaming but it was clearly understood that this was the last day of project Brexit. Then a call from Stuart Scotland, he had gone to the station expecting to find me there leafleting. It was half six and I was due in

Moulscombe at seven. The baby was crying. I backed out of the door still apologising.

I ran up the hill to meet Stuart. We shook hands. I explained that Anne had told everyone to not target the stations as that might incentivise the opposition so instead I was off to Molescombe.

He asked if I had any leaflets, I said no but I had loads at home. He asked if it was near, it was but I just couldn't go back to the house with Stuart to rifle through the boxes with Vicky there feeding our daughter and the ceiling dripping. Stuart had to be in Tunbridge Wells by 9 anyway so we shook hands. It was 6:45 so I jumped in a cab.

Got to Molescombe Way on time, but still with no breakfast. Ian was there with John Kelly who I recognised as he had picked up leaflets from the house a couple of times. There were a couple of builders there, we asked them if they were anything to do with the referendum, they replied definitely not. Ian quipped that we were just waiting for the leader, I phoned Tom just as his camper van turned into Molescombe Way.

Ian huffed *'is this all there is?'* And he was right, there were only four of us. That was when I saw what a mistake I had made with the stall. Instead of shouting out clever slogans on the other side of the street, I should have stayed close to the table and written people's email addresses and phone numbers down clearly on the clip board. We should have used the stall to build a big reservoir of volunteers instead of remaining a small number of obsessive eccentric nutters. If I had seen that at the beginning we wouldn't have had to rely on the energy of a small number of enthusiasts at the end.

We looked at the houses, it was a desolate place. Tom said something about how the people here had been left behind. We weren't sure what we were doing or where to go. Only Tom had brought one small map. In the end, Ian and I did the roads off one side of Molescombe Way, Tom and John did the other.

Molescombe is hell, England flags, Rottweilers, bits of rusty bikes in the front gardens. It's a dumping ground. Worst of all every house has a really long front garden path! The thinking was that if everyone who supported us actually bothered to vote for us then we would win so it wasn't about winning arguments or changing minds anymore but getting the vote out. The leaflets we delivered said 'TODAY IS POLLING DAY' and contained a few basic facts.

I'm a bit shy and don't like disturbing people so I would tentatively put the leaflets in which would crumple up on the draft excluders or get caught in the flap so they didn't drop right down to the floor. So, I gave myself a bit of a talking to – I was 47 years old and I found myself in the arse end of nowhere delivering maps of Turkey at 7:30 with no breakfast, in the rain. I hadn't walked all the way up that rubbish strewn path to just leave the information crumpled in the draft excluders! I had to be sure every leaflet dropped down, so I pushed them right in.

It's tempting to say the least effective work I did was when I acted on orders from central command and the work we did as a self-organising nobodies was better, but it's horses for courses. The Molescombe work was not a waste of time because these really were our core voters and they were also the sort of people who might have forgotten to vote, and in a 50/50 contest a 1% swing is everything.

It was now raining heavily, I felt we hadn't done enough streets but Ian decided to head back to his car. Finally, we got some food from the shop, we stood together in the rain in silence, but even then, neither of us actually said the words *"do you think we will win?"* Ian just said, *"if we don't win I will be so depressed"* and I agreed. John and Tom met us. I wasn't sure if we had finished for the day and felt we should do more but Ian offered me a lift home so I thought, ok take the lift and do the station again in the afternoon. In the car we were quiet, I kept thinking, *'have I done enough?'*

I took Jnr down to the polling station, it all seemed in order, no Remainers campaigning outside. I joked with the two ladies there that it was strange to give an affirmative vote with a 'X' and that maybe it should be a tick instead? They reassured me that you definitely put a 'X' by the option that you *do* want. I tried to focus on the voting paper, leave was definitely the second one, at the bottom of the page. I voted with tears in my eyes. Jnr was trying to climb on the voting booth.

Joy! It was a thunder storm and low turnout favours the side that is most motivated to vote. Unfortunately, the storm finished in Brighton at six as people were returning from work, but it was still raining in London which was a strong Remain area. So, the rain was a good sign, although Vicky didn't quite see it that way as she rearranged the buckets in the kitchen.

I put one last post on Facebook:

"Tony Benn said that democracy was when a little old lady could go into a voting booth, put an 'X' in a box and

overthrow the government. That is what I voted for today, it is horrifying how totally this referendum has been misunderstood. A neoliberal tyranny has masqueraded as a progressive friend of workers and the environment, and has bought off public opinion with grants to its carefully selected stooges. It's opponents (myself included) have been traduced as flat-earth knuckle-draggers. Yesterday I campaigned outside Brighton station for 12 hours, someone called me a murderer. At one point six Green Party campaigners surrounded me and started berating me. My opinion of them is that they are the useful idiots of a regime that shares none of their (laudable) concerns. It's been a lonely campaign, thank goodness I have a wonderful wife. That said some Remainers have bothered to make intelligent well-informed points that I respectfully disagree with. If Britain actually votes to NOT govern itself I will be inconsolable. But if the voters throw off all the state-sponsored paranoia and character assassinations and propaganda masquerading as objective information and vote for functional independent government then there will be no celebrating or gloating from me. I will just quietly and with much relief get back on with my life. Either way I will always know I could not have done any more."

I saw I had some replies from the usual interlocutors. I was scared of reading them, what could they have written? Probably some devastating argument exposing me as monstrous. I eventually looked and every one was gracious.

John Paul O'Neill: *'I thought you'd already written your last post?* 😑 *I am just off to cancel out your vote! Whatever way it goes I hope to see you again soon doing a bit of poeting!* JP'

127

John Lyons: *'Whilst I didn't vote the way you did, I am as ever impressed with the passion and integrity you've displayed in making the case. I'll be glad when this whole vindictive mess is over, it's been a sorry campaign from all sides and has done little to represent the country I'm proud of. Whichever way it goes it won't be the end of the world, and if it doesn't go your way don't stay inconsolable for long. Respect.'*

Laurence Owen: *'I've been following your blogs and updates silently and I've definitely found them to be the most eloquent and sensible leave arguments I've seen. I am, in the end, a Remainer, but thank you for speaking sense! Hope all' swell with you.'*

Toby McCulloch: *'As someone else put it ... "Voting out is like telling your parents you want independence and moving into the garage..."'*

Neil Sheppeck: *'Whichever half of the country doesn't get the majority, I hope they'll respect the democratic process. I share your passion albeit for a different result, and hope to share a pint and a laugh with you soon x'*

Johnny Rocket: *'Love you Seb, but I've seen inside Bojo's heart and he's a mean-spirited demigod. One form of tyranny or another...I like my future to have no borders, nationalism or an anachronistic pack of Oxbridge elitists squabbling over which right wing graduate runs the UK. I after all am immigrant from outside the EU who has never collected the dole, a grant, paid taxes, collect VAT and always promoted UK talent. I am the unacceptable face of immigration for these xenophobes. I of course will always call you friend but you're buying the next round ♥ '*

Sebastian Handley: *'Stop it – you guys are making me cry and we haven't even had the results yet!'*

John Lyons: *'Shut up murderer'*

Johnny Rocket: *'You'll be crying into that huge pint (0.5682623 litres EU) of beer you'll be buying me.'*

Len Richardson: *'You're wrong but for the right reasons.'*

Annette Richardson: *'You do have a wonderful wife.'*

Len Richardson: *'If she was that wonderful she would have hidden his pen!'*

I toyed with the idea of going to *'central command'* (Anne's House) to call supporters to check they voted but instead I went to pick up Jnr from nursery. I felt the way I always feel when I leave a job – that I wished I had done more.

Pushing the pram back home as I crossed the road, in the distance I thought I saw Nihal the Punk Poet, one of the best poets I had seen in the last few years. I hurried on. If he was pissed off with me for my posts on Facebook then I didn't want to embarrass him by stopping to say *'hi'*.

I phoned mum and dad and Iona (my grown-up daughter) to check they had voted. I contacted Anne about going to the Corn Exchange to help oversee the count but she said I hadn't given her the necessary details in time so I couldn't attend. I can't remember what else I did until the polls closed (10pm) probably ranting on Facebook, but for me, at last, the war was over.

I sat in bed at ten and the last few polls were showing us losing 48/52. It was pretty clear to me what or rather who had lost it for us – Thomas Mair. I posted on Facebook blaming him for our defeat and wishing him a long and miserable incarceration. Then I checked the press, Gibraltar was an early declaration, rock solid remain (sorry). Paul Perrin tweeted he hoped Spain would invade them. Up to now the war had been fought on Facebook but now Twitter took over as the page to check. Newcastle had just called for remain but the swing was much smaller than expected. Probably just a one off. People were tweeting that Sunderland was the next one to watch, then Sunderland called it 61/39 for leave. Holy fucking cow, there really *was* hope! Sterling dropped 3% in a couple of minutes, bookmakers shortened their odds. One by one as the results came in a trend became apparent, the pollsters had underestimated the support for the unfashionable side by about 4% (told you so). I tweeted that I would pay anything to see a picture of Cameron's face right now. Jennifer Lyons replied that I could pay £10,000 for it if I wanted because it would only be worth 20p soon the way Sterling was going. Vicky told me to get some sleep but a revolution was unfolding on Twitter. All bookies were now predicting a vote to leave and we were now in the lead, but ominously no London borough had called yet and tweeters were predicting a 400% turnout in Tower Hamlets. Then Lambeth called. A huge margin for Remain taking them back into the lead. I decided to leave it finely balanced and call it a day.

Text from Wayne: *"Love and Peace xxx"*

Friday 24th June
I tried to make out my phone screen, there was sleep in my eyes and some of the text on the Guardian website was yellow. I looked and looked. It was 5:30 with still some constituencies to declare. But at 4:40 am the Leave vote had become unassailable. We had declared independence.

I sat on the side of the bed with my back to Vicky, who was sleeping and I cried a bit, but it was more a sort of cough/sob - not much of a celebration I suppose. I took a few deep breaths, and thought to myself *'thank god it's over'*. I walked around the bed and sat next to Vicky and told her we had won, and that I loved her and thanked her for standing by me.

We dun 'em. The whole of the establishment thought that so long as they scared us enough we would put up with their shit no matter how shit it was, but a load of self-organizing nobodies up and down the country had changed the course of history. But then Vicky said she was picking up a lot of recrimination on Facebook, the backlash had begun already. I took the Tony Benn poster and the Vote Leave stickers out of the window straight away. I posted *'if you can't join them, beat them'*. On Facebook but then deleted it as there were some very angry people out there.

Walking from my house to the train station it felt like I was breathing fresh air for the first time in my life, there seemed to be a slight haze, I was almost stumbling, dazed that it was finally over. I walked past the van man delivering his bread as usual, the newsagent was taking in his papers, it was Thomas Hardy's *'In Time of "The Breaking of Nations"'*. Across the planet world leaders were staring at their computer screens open mouthed as I quietly plodded up the hill. That walk from home to the station was the one time I truly felt at peace.

Text from Wayne: *"yes yes fucking yes X"*

Texted Paul: *"God bless you sir. We done 'em. You're a national hero"*

Texted Tom: *"God bless you sir! You are the future of the Labour Party. We done em. Cameron and UKIP are now finished. It's the beginning of a new age."*

Tom replied: *"Well done Seb. What a momentous night for our country. Here's to being a self-governing democracy again!"*

Counter-Revolution:
The Consequences of Victory.

Well, the future didn't turn out how I expected ...

I got on the train and Tony was there. I should have sat in another carriage till the whole mood of the country had calmed down, but I sat diagonally opposite and we jokingly cringed at one another. Coming from Northern Ireland and working at the National Theatre (which probably receives EU funding) there was every possibility that he would have reasonable concerns, as the ramifications for the Irish border and arts funding were completely unknown quantities. We joked about it a bit and I feigned disinterest in all that boring political stuff, and mentioned that it also meant the end of Cameron, Osborne, UKIP and Farage which was a pretty big silver lining!

Iona called and I whispered I couldn't talk because I was on the train. She asked what had happened. I fought back the tears and whispered, *"we done 'em"* she cheered. Thankfully I don't think Tony heard! I worked out how to suspend my Facebook account from my phone and checked the BBC news.

Cameron was resigning, I didn't catch it from the beginning but it was the most gracious speech I had ever heard him make, and for the first time I admired him. There was however one quibble I had with his statement, although it didn't seem much at the time, he said: *"I was absolutely clear about my belief that Britain is stronger safer and better off inside the European Union."*

Ok even if he thought this was true, this was not the time to say those words, what confidence would the markets have if our own Prime Minister was declaring to the world that we had made a catastrophic error? Saying that independence was the wrong choice was the sort of thing to come out with before the vote not after. A better approach would have been to say that his dire warnings were made in the heat of the campaign, that deep down he was confident any turbulence would be temporary, that the fundamentals were sound, and that a contingency plan was in hand. It would have been a climb down, but hey, he was resigning anyway! That would have been the right thing to do for the country, if not his legacy. Think about it, for the first time in our history our leaders had a vested interest in our economy doing badly. The Prime Minister, Chancellor of the Exchequer and Governor of the Bank of England had campaigned against what was now official government policy, so the worse the economy got, the more they appeared to be vindicated, conversely the better the economy got the more ridiculous their pre-poll predictions of economic armageddon looked. It's called a conflict of interest and it didn't help that the Labour party also appeared to be at war with itself, with its heartlands voting for Brexit and its MPs voting for Remain. Lame duck Prime Minister, lame duck Chancellor, lame duck Leader of the Opposition, the Queen was 90, who the fuck was running the country? Mark Carney? The Pound dropped 20%. Could it get any worse? Yes.

I sat in the cafe and got a text from an old friend: *"are you fucking happy now?!?!"* The backlash was well and truly underway.

Making a tea in the kitchen, I bumped into a work colleague, someone I had been to lunch with a couple of times, and one of a handful of co-workers who was also a Facebook *'friend'* It felt awkward and I wasn't sure if she had tears in her eyes.

"Sorry if I've been ranting on Facebook."

"That's ok I blocked it some time ago."

I asked something about the elections in her native Australia. She said something about the whole world becoming less caring.

I shouldn't have gone into work that day, the sense of righteous anger was palpable, I noticed one person was going to walk past me but then took a different path, was it that they didn't want to acknowledge me? Group emails went around about what a sad day it was, always making the assumption that everyone addressed was a sophisticated modern *'progressive'* who deplored this *'lurch to the right'*. This had always been the Remain approach, to present themselves as the defenders of lofty values and publicly assume that those of a different persuasion were mentally ill/racist/parochial/fantasists etc, but now it was supercharged with shock and indignation.

One boss openly speculated that those who voted Brexit should get a pay cut because those who didn't shouldn't have to bear the consequences of the downturn that would follow. I thought this was an excellent idea because, by precisely the same reasoning, when the economy experienced the *'Brexit Boom'* that would mean I'd be entitled to a huge bonus! But I kept my mouth shut.

At six I went straight home. Vicky had been crying. She couldn't suspend her Facebook account because she needed it for her marketing work and all our friends had been saying Brexiters were racist. A dear old friend of mine had said we were *"the great unwashed"*. People who were in our wedding photos were publicly traumatised and venting their spleens in our general direction. My lot had killed Bambi's mum. Vicky asked me if I was sure we had done the right thing. I replied I was stone cold certain. Vicky said she felt very alone, that she wasn't as strong as me and she thought it was all supposed to be over.

During the campaign, you are braced for attacks and you soldier on. It's tough, it's bruising but you look to the finishing line, put on a brave face and plod forwards. But once you've won, mustering the tiniest bit of energy to keep going is very difficult. For months, we had been looking forward to the day when we didn't have to argue or check the polls anymore, so once we had won all the Brexit groups just evaporated as the entire establishment, furious, energised (and still in power!) began a campaign to steal our revolution.

I can't speak for the rest but deep down I was never confident we would win so I'm guessing Remain never really believed they would lose, so when it actually happened everyone was in shock. I had always assumed that I would be the embittered loser attributing all the ills of the modern world to the Remainers, I never imagined it would end up the other way round. So, there are actually disadvantages to winning because winning means you own all the consequences of the decision, whereas losing exonerates you from blame for anything and gives you a convenient repository of blame for all the ills of the world.

So, this would be another titbit of advice to all you would-be revolutionaries out there – don't think it's over once you've won. Don't dissolve your organisations and don't stop campaigning because the old guard will seek to steal your revolution.

Writing in the Guardian Poly Toynbee gave her verdict: *"Catastrophe. Britain has broken apart ... as treasury receipts fall, there will be less of everything."* We had given the EU 43 years but in under 43 hours it had been decided that independence was a disaster.

Saturday 25th June

What unfolded next was the biggest howl of anguish in British political history.

I had virtually stopped checking my phone but while taking Jnr to the park I scanned the Guardian website. A petition calling for a second referendum had attracted a record 400,000 signatures, and it wasn't just a call for a second referendum: *'We the undersigned call upon HM Government to implement a rule that if the remain or leave vote is less than 60% based on a turnout of less than 75% there should be another referendum. '*

Britain's electorate is 45 million, so a 75% turnout would be 33.75 million people (It's very rare for elections to have a turnout as high as 75% – the referendum we had just had was the biggest vote in British history and even that was only a 72.2% turnout). But let's say there *was* a second referendum and 75% of the electorate actually voted (unlikely). 60% of 33.75 million is 20.25 million people. So, Leave would need at least 20.25 million votes to win that referendum, whereas Remain would only require 13.5 million votes to keep their system in place!

Some re-match, not content with a sloping pitch they were proposing different sized goals and a one-eyed ref just to make sure – as if they didn't have the odds stacked in their favour enough the first time! If such a system were used in a general election the government would never ever change, which of course was the whole point. There was only one word to describe the proposal: conservative. They were seeking to annul an entirely legitimate referendum that was fairly won on a high turnout, on their terms, and replace it with a pseudo-democracy hard-wired to prevent change. If it were not so nakedly mendacious it would be laughable, but hey, that's Euro *'democracy*' for you! How did they have the gall to even call it a *'second referendum'* when what they were really demanding was either a third referendum or a coup d'etat?

Meanwhile in cities across Britain the horrifying rise of the far right had begun. Thousands of demonstrators were marching in London, Birmingham, Edinburgh, Oxford and Cambridge calling for the Government to not trigger Article 50 (the formal mechanism for leaving). In London David Lammy, Tim Farron, and (predictably) Bob Geldof all made speeches about why the referendum result should be disregarded. From Paris, renowned cartographer Jarvis Cocker released a video message saying *"you cannot deny geography. The U.K. is in Europe "*.

A breakdown of the vote had emerged. England and Wales had voted out, Scotland and London had voted in but with low turnouts, Northern Ireland was mixed but overall 56% remain. The old had voted out and the young had voted in. The better educated to remain, the less well educated to leave. The more wealthy to remain, the less wealthy to leave. Here is how the conservatives interpreted the vote breakdown:

March for Europe organiser Mark Thomas: *"We would accept the result of the referendum if it was fought on a level playing field, but it was full of misinformation"*

Ahh so the vote shouldn't count because we were too ignorant...

Bob Geldof: *"oh shame on you. Shame on you* [older Brexit voters] *you robbed the young of their future."*

Ahh, so the vote shouldn't count because we were the wrong age...

David Lammy: *"If the UK leaves the European Union the break-up of the union will swiftly follow if Scotland gains independence. Are we ready and willing to dismantle our nation? We weren't asked this and it was not a factor widely considered on Thursday ... The referendum was non-binding ... It's not too late to stop this"*

Ahh so Welsh votes can be ignored, and English votes can be ignored, but Scottish votes can't? The ramifications were not widely considered enough? Well then maybe Remain should have spent the last six months presenting clear arguments rather than hysterical conjecture, calling us bigots and manically repeating *'more in common'*. So *'it's not too late to stop this?'* You mean it's ok to just ignore the biggest and most democratic vote in British history?

Well, thank goodness the progressives heroically stood against the far right!

Imagine for a moment that Remain had won with 52% of the vote. And imagine that having lost the vote, an unrepresentative group of public figures claimed that the result was merely advisory and not legally binding, so they went ahead and triggered Article 50 anyway. Well I'm asking you to imagine that, but you can't, I can't, no one can, it's totally inconceivable that Article 50 would have been triggered if Britain had voted to remain. And yet precisely such an outrage was actually being discussed!

Let's put it another way...

Attlee won a landslide with 11.9 million votes.
Thatcher won a landslide with 13.7 million votes.
Major set a record of 14.1 million votes.
Blair won a landslide with 13.5 million votes.
Brexit had smashed all records with over 17.4 million votes.

401 constituencies voted to leave, 231 to remain, but people were actually campaigning *against* its recognition! And they weren't even being embarrassed or apologetic about it – they were actually marching through the streets with painted faces and flags shouting for the vote to be disregarded! ... and claiming to be *'progressive'*! ... and with straight faces they actually complained that the nation was *'divided'* and that there had been a *'lurch to the right'*! Their hypocrisy was breathtaking.

Ok so I think they were the far right, and they probably think I was, so who was ... er ... right?

Well, for a start they were conservatives. Not just because they wanted to conserve the existing system, but because the system they wanted to conserve was itself specifically designed to be unreformable.

Next, Remain always took the path of least democracy. They did everything they could to prevent a referendum in the first place. When they couldn't prevent the vote they complained it was *'destabilising'*. When they lost it they campaigned for it to be disregarded. The only time they wanted a referendum they proposed it be rigged so they couldn't lose it.

Can I give another example? Yes. The argument that we should stay in the EU because it gives us better laws, automatically falls down because an independent Britain can pass whatever laws it wants – laws identical to EU laws if we like – the only precondition is that now we will have to actually *vote* for them first. Why would they be against that? There was only one explanation: they wanted laws people would not *vote* for.

Can I give another example? Yes. We campaigned flat out *before* the vote, whereas they campaigned flat out *after* the vote.

Can I give another example? Yes. The Brexiteers campaign was primarily about the referendum where everyone could participate and every vote counted equally, whereas Remain repeatedly sought to move the process to smaller, less representative institutions, stacked with political appointees like the High Court or the House of Lords.

Can I give another example? Yes. Just like the EU itself, at every turn they sought to move decision making above the heads of voters.

They sought to annul the vote for the '*greater good*' of EU membership whilst we sought to annul our EU membership for the greater good of being democratic. So, we see a consistent pattern of behaviour running through everything they do – whatever situation they are confronted with the Euro apologists always always advocate the path of least democracy, and their conduct at this time confirmed the opinion I always had of Remain – that authoritarianism was not some unfortunate by-product of their beliefs but the foundation of them, which is why they had to be defeated at all costs.

Ahh but couldn't they accuse me of being a nationalist? I suppose they could if they wanted (even though I have never waved a Union Jack or sung the national anthem in my life) and their accusation would be hypocrisy anyway because Remain supporters *are* nationalist patriots who believe themselves to be citizens of a nation called the EU, which has its own flag, parliament, judiciary, anthem, president, constitution, and legal system and which will soon have its own army. Remain supporters were actually marching through the streets waving flags. How is that not nationalism?

Here is a photo of the March for Europe...down with nationalism yeah?

Trawling through the various speeches and articles written at this time by Toynbee, Farron, Lammy etc. it's astonishing how emotive and fact free they were. Virtually every one assumed there would be a huge Brexit recession that would hit the poor the most, as immigrants were burned at the stake, universities closed, the nation collapsed and children scavenged for food.

Generally, their impassioned rhetoric was inversely proportional to their factual content. Why was this? Could it be that the vehemence with which they advanced their case hid a deeper insecurity? That actually they weren't trying to convince us anymore, but themselves? Why didn't they just calmly present a reasonable argument for EU membership *before* the vote rather than an impassioned defence of it afterwards? My theory, which you are welcome to disregard, is it's because *'Europe'* was no longer a political idea but a religious belief. The Remain campaign was a classic example of conservatives accusing empiricists of heresy. (See also 14th May)

Supporters of the EU were everything they claimed to despise: angry, irrational, conservative, nationalists who attacked democracy with unfalsifiable pseudo-science. Welcome to the new fascism.

So, if you watch a film like Return of the Jedi, Total Recall or the Running Man, at the end when the grip of the empire is finally broken, everyone has a party, and there's a big bonfire and drinks and singing and people hugging. Well that's exactly what *wasn't* happening. These were dark days when I felt total powerlessness and disillusionment, that having given everything and triumphing against the odds some technicality was going to be produced to annul the result. Even the US Secretary of State John Kerry was openly speculating that Brexit might be *'walked back'*, and with the evaporation of the Brexit groups all we could do was hope that an establishment which totally disagreed with us, respected democracy enough to follow our instruction.

It was like winning the marathon only to be told that the race would never actually end. It was like Leicester City winning the Premiership only to be told they had scored *'the wrong type of goals'*. How many more examples do I have to give? Why am I even having to explain that the vote should be respected and that democracy is important? Because *that* was the horrifying enormity of the coup the conservatives were trying to get away with! For Remain to win democracy had to lose and they were well organised, well funded, highly motivated and well connected. It was a national crisis.

Monday 27th June

The petition to hold a second referendum was now at about 3 million votes and back at the office there were no shortage of people eager to forward the petition link around. All morning the students were emailing (copying me in) about how important it was to share the link, then the associates started pitching in too, cc'ing the whole office. Again, I didn't take the bait of replying, even though by now it was an open secret I was Brexit. It's not that they would sack me – they were decent conscientious professionals, the best employers anyone could wish for – but with a wife and three children to support why risk an argument?

Ok, to summarise: In the Kubler Ross model there are five stages of grief:
1, Denial
2, Anger
3, Bargaining

4, Depression

5, Acceptance

Basically, at this time there was an excess of numbers one to four and a distinct lack of number five. The entire country was in limbo, the Prime Minister was a lame duck, the Chancellor was a lame duck, Labour were in the middle of a leadership election, no one in the world knew where Britain's laws would be written in 25 months' time and the Queen was 90. Anyone working in the financial markets would be entirely within their rights to ask *'who the fuck is running the country?'* To his credit Mark Carney had back-pedalled on the scare stories and was doing his best to calm the markets, but the act of government was simply not happening. At PMQs Cameron answered every question with the response that it would be for the next Prime Minister to decide, not him. So, what the hell *was* his job if not to steer us through this? But encouragement came from an unlikely source – European leaders themselves had no appetite for another year of pre-referendum uncertainty and urged Britain to trigger Article 50 without delay – they were actually right about something!

That night England lost to Iceland 2:1 in Euro 2016. It was widely regarded to be the worst England defeat of all time – and that's saying something!

Tuesday 28th June
I emailed the students in the office (not the bosses)

Iceland V England. We demand a rematch!
Please sign this petition demanding that the Iceland V England game be replayed for the following reasons:

The score of 2:1 is a difference of only one goal which isn't really a proper victory.

Many of the England players were confused and didn't actually know what they were doing.

Iceland's strategy was blatantly 'Anglo-phobic' taking the ball, keeping it all for themselves, and then kicking it directly AT the England goal, resulting in the incorrect distribution of points.

Iceland is a small parochial island and as such does not deserve to progress.

If things are decided simply on the basis of score achieved then that will destabilise the pre-ordained order of things causing uncertainty and anarchy! Therefore, we the undersigned insist that the match be replayed with different sized goals until the correct result is achieved.

A few managed unamused responses. I was too exhausted look at Facebook or Twitter anymore but I also emailed it round to some friends. Nick responded *"but football doesn't matter anymore now British life is just one big Countryside Alliance march."*

The mood of national mourning showed few signs of abating. The petition for a second referendum had by now received about four million signatures.

Wednesday 29th June

Ok so the Brighton Brexiteers had helped bring about the biggest political upset of the modern age, but could we organise a piss-up in a pub? Apparently not! Various dates and pubs were mooted but we were all so busy with what had been neglected, it wasn't till today that Ian grabbed the bull by the horns and declared that we were all meeting at the Yeoman on Saturday at midday.

The rest of us agreed this was a good idea. Not the sort of guy to order a salad.

Thursday 30th June

A day of high political drama! Michael Gove brutally sabotaged Boris Johnson's leadership bid and put himself forward to be the next leader of the Tory party and PM. Journalists quoted Julius Caesar and Macbeth. Why had Gove, a man who had nine times ruled himself out of contention for leadership, supplanted the person he was actually campaigning for just the night before? Clearly behind the squeaky voice and Rick Moranis appearance there was ice.

I walked with a spring in my step, clearly he was a shit, but he was *our* shit. Johnson was a great character during the campaign but could not have been trusted to complete our revolution and Theresa May had voted Remain. The only leadership contender who believed in independence on principal was Gove. So, whilst the journalists cited Machiavelli I saw Gove's *'treachery'* as a genuine act of reluctance – he saw that if that moment had not been seized the whole battle could have been for nothing. So long as Gove made it to the last two it would go to the party membership who would surely elect him over May. Yes, Theresa May would be more likely to win an election. But I don't give a crap about this or that party – I give a crap that elections are meaningful.

Friday 1st July

Arch europhile Ken Clarke calls on Gove to quit the race. Tony Blair angles for job as Brexit negotiator. Talk about poacher turned gamekeeper! The entire establishment was manoeuvring to steal our revolution...And now Gove had revealed himself as an assassin a new theory came into play – that the one who wields the knife never becomes king. But surely it must be Gove? Well so I thought only eight hours previously but now apparently, he wouldn't invoke Article 50 till 2017 either. And what's this? Rank outsider Andrea Leadsom says she would trigger Article 50 immediately and is already ahead of Gove with the bookies! It's always the one that comes from nowhere....

A rival petition was up, with 700 signatures calling for Article 50 to be triggered immediately. I emailed and tweeted it to the world and his dog straightaway; got back onto Facebook, sent the petition link to various Brexit groups then suspended my Facebook again. By the train journey home it was over 4,000.

Decent but with the Remain petition now at 4 million anything less than 100,000 would feel like a defeat.

Saturday 2nd July
I met Ian at the Yeoman. As the others turned up one by one I asked *"so – have we won?"* Their responses ranged from optimistic certainty (Vicki) to brooding pessimism (Ian). Peter was circumspect, Wayne just laughed. Paul seemed relieved but was concerned that the negotiation would be a dog's dinner, I questioned whether that was really a problem, could we not just sort out any remaining issues election by election? His misgiving was that in theory we could, but that in practice, just like the Barnett Formula with Scotland, unsatisfactory compromises had a habit of becoming permanent. A fair observation, but at least if we tolerated a bad deal

it would be because we put up with it and not because it was imposed on us.

Monday 11th July

Andrea Leadsom pulls out of the race. It will be a May coronation. At lunch-time I joined UKIP. They promptly collapsed.

Wednesday 13th July

Theresa May becomes Prime Minister.

Text from Nick: *"Sorry to hear about your mate Leadsom"*.

So, the Labour and Tory parties had been holding leadership elections concurrently, but why was it that while it took Labour all summer to re-elect the same leader, the Tories changed the guard in just twenty days of brutal political bloodletting? There are better placed commentators than myself to speculate but I suspect it's this: because no two people will have quite the same political beliefs, when it comes to a matter of principal like independence, if you doubt that your political ally is ideologically pure you cannot take any chances – you are duty bound to immediately neutralise them whatever the cost. Which is why the Brexit Tories immediately turned on one another.

Thursday 21st July

Bumped into John Kapp at Brighton station and asked him about his run-in with the law: *"I was caught white-handed!"* I asked if he thought we had won, he replied *"undoubtedly"* adding that the 24th of June was the happiest day of his life. I'm guessing that John was born in the early 1940s so if it really was the happiest day of his life then that made it number one of about 30,000. Either way I wish him many more happy days.

Text from Nick: *'I notice you are following Farage on Twitter'*
I replied: *'...couldn't find Satan...'*

August to September
As the weeks went by Theresa May acted methodically, she swiftly dispensed with various ministers from privileged public school backgrounds and I craved a similarly ruthless defenestration of the Remainers, and it came, but agonisingly slowly. One by one the Remain bridgeheads were shut off: no there would not be a second referendum, no Scotland would not have a veto, no remaining in the single market was not sacrosanct and no we would not wait till after the French and German elections. I studied the body language of David Davies, Liam Fox and Boris Johnson, the new Brexit ministers, they seemed relaxed and cheerful, was it finally really over?

Meanwhile *'the post-Brexit recession'* which George Osborne, David Lammy Christine Lagarde, Tim Farron, Polly Toynbee, Paul Collier (etc. etc. etc.) assured us would happen, was conspicuous by its absence. The UK service sector grew 0.4% in July, much more strongly than expected. The OECD (who had predicted a post-Brexit recession) revised its UK 2016 growth forecasts up from 1.7 to 1.8%. Whilst Remain valiantly clung to the line that the weaker pound was the same thing as a weaker economy, exports, tourism and inward investment surged: GSK invested £275 million, Wells Fargo £300 million, AstraZeneca £330 million, SoftBank £24.3 billion. The house price crash predicted by George Osborne simply failed to happen, in fact there was a slight rise in transactions in August. Additionally, Osborne's threatened punitive emergency budget was a no show and his prediction that every family would be £4,300 per year worse off was quietly forgotten. Recruitment agencies reported a boom.

Start-ups were launched at a faster rate after the vote than before it. Within 100 days, consumer confidence had jumped six points to surpass pre-referendum levels and even the (EU funded) IMF conceded that Britain was the fastest growing of the G7 economies. Ten year bond yields (traditionally an indicator of risk) sank below 1%.

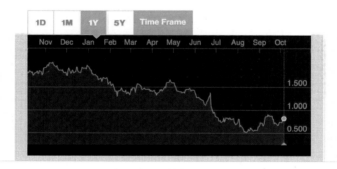

"The Purchasing Managers Index rose to 55.4 in September ... beating market expectations ... it was the highest reading since June 2014, as growth of output new orders and employment all strengthened" – Trading Economics.

Here I can do no better than quote Dan Hannan who was brilliant throughout the campaign:

"We were told the stock exchange would collapse. It did – the Italian stock exchange – British stocks were the best performing in Europe."

My perfectly sensible observation (3rd March) that as an independent nation Britain would enjoy a GDP approximately double that of the Eurozone and unemployment about half that of the Eurozone was inaccurate only in-so-far as it underestimated the harvest independence would reap. Here is the FTSE All Share index over the last year, we can clearly see the blip that happened on 24th June, but look at what happened next – call that a recession?

Ahh but the FTSE All Share index is a domestic barometer, what about the FTSE 250 which is more international in its outlook? Well that looks even healthier! ...

As usual Remainers based their pessimism on unfalsifiable conjecture, surveys, and forecasts, so the vindicating crash they yearned for was always just around the corner. The actual figures however were relentlessly benign, it was our description of them as *'project fear'* that was vindicated – they had been making it up all along.

I emailed Jordan to tell him I was writing a book about Brexit, and asked if I could mention him and whether he had any idea how many hits my essays had.

He confirmed his name was Jordan Ganner and the stats were about ten times what I was expecting: *"Total Facebook reach for your articles was 521,000 – google analytics shows 137,839 converted into readers from Facebook and visited GBrexit.com to read the full articles."*

Saturday. 24th September
Jeremy Corbyn re-elected Labour leader. He voted remain and advocated remain but never attended one Labour EU Remain meeting, whichever side you are on its undeniable that he just didn't lead. Just like Theresa May and Phillip Hammond, when the hour came he simply didn't stand for what he believed in, which is I suppose why they are at the top and I am organising bathroom schedules. So my next tip is – if you want to get to the top then don't be like me!

October 2016
Personally, it is my view that independence was declared on 23rd June 2016 and that Article 50 is just a piece of foreign law irrelevant to Britain. But although I disagree, let's assume that Article 50 is the way independence will be done. All Theresa May

had to do was write one letter to end the uncertainty and move on. But did she seize the moment? No, her government spent the next few months pontificating about what negotiating strategy it should adopt in the two years after it was triggered. This allowed the anti-democrats to begin their disgraceful legal attempt to stop the referendum result from being enacted. (Naturally as they did so they claimed to be the heroic upholders of decency) So as May vacillated the prospect emerged of independence having to navigate a Kafkaesque legal odyssey through the High Court, the Supreme Court, the European Court (?!) the Commons (again) and the Lords (again!). Why didn't she just spend one hour writing one letter on day one? Why didn't Cameron?

My blood boiled as appointees from pygmy institutions like the High Court, the House of Lords and the Supreme Court had the temerity to act as if our Declaration of Independence was something they were somehow entitled to approve or interpret. How could they not see that the *truly* supreme body had *already* delivered it's judgement?

Well I could go on and on with an endless running commentary on the continuing developments but there are others better placed than myself to record these, and realistically the story of *'David Cameron - My Part In His Downfall'* ended on June 23rd. So again with the situation finely balanced I will call it a day. Will the conservatives somehow manage to steal the revolution and realise their dream of a Britain in which only meaningless votes are allowed?

Will it end in a shabby compromise, riots or a civil war? Everyone imagined it would be like a quiz show, cup final, or general election where time is called, points tallied and the prize duly awarded, but the absence of a fat lady singing means that to this day I have never raised a glass to victory. But if, when, Article 50 is triggered you will find me with my folding table and steadfast friends on Brexit Corner giving out free fruit cake, and every June 23rd thereafter. And if representative democracy is snuffed out, it won't be because courage failed the people, but because courage failed our leaders.

Conclusion

The two sides were the embodiments of their respective philosophies. On the Remain side there was a centrally organised, top-down command structure that gave instructions to their local groups (the way the EU 'works') Whilst on the independence side there were lots of uncoordinated, half-decent autonomous groups cooperating with one another (the way Europe *should* work).

Lining up for Remain was the entire establishment: Cameron, Obama, Legarde, Carney, Osborne, Corbyn, Merkel, Hollande, Junker, Schultz, Blair, Brown, Clegg, Major, Tusk, the BOE, the CBI, the TUC, the IMF, the IFS, the BBC, the OECD, the LSE, even David Beckham! And on the independence side there were the misfits, the rejects, the outcasts, the mavericks, the failures, the nutters, and the fruitcakes.

They said *'the experts know best'*, but we rightly doubted their sincerity and impartiality.

They sought to confuse with technicalities and jargon, we sought to explain with examples.

They said *'listen'*. We said *'look'*.

They beat us in the gated media, while we did better on Facebook, Twitter and the chat forums.

They talked about independence in a negative way, we talked about it in a positive way.

They thought it was about what laws are written, we knew it as about *how* laws are written.

They said *'don't change'*. We said *'change'*.

They said *'be scared'*. We said *'don't be scared'*.

They campaigned after the vote. We campaigned before the vote.

They were professionals, we were amateurs.

They were cool, we were uncool.

They had a strategy, we didn't.

They had leaders, we didn't.

They were the alpha males, the presidents, the governors, the experts, the insiders, the employers, the somebodies. We were the nobodies.

The winners lost and the losers won. It was the victory of empiricism over a vast institutionalised delusion. And when it was all over they went back to their somebody jobs and talked about how they saw it, and we went back to our nobody jobs and listened to them.

In terms of raw Machiavellian politics I would say that the Remain campaign was fairly good before the vote, and very good after the vote. Their two most effective strategies were:

1, Making it an anti-social thought crime to disagree with them, because that pre-emptively silenced so many of our arguments.

2, Funding campaign groups to act as their stooges within the media, because this created a wall of pseudo-objective pro-EU propaganda (See 23rd May).

This was cynical, but even I must concede it was politically brilliant.

I would say there were only three things the Remain campaign got wrong:

1, Too monolithic, too centrally organised, they weren't ideologically broad-based enough.

2, Poor ground campaign. They focused on dominating the main stream media where they were already strong. So, they ended up talking to themselves rather than reaching out to ordinary people.

3, Shit product. I can't put it any kinder than that. Their campaign was actually fairly strong but when you have such a bag of crap for sale, however passionately you flog it, there are only going to be so many people weak, scared or stupid enough to buy it. From Obama to Mair, everything went *right* for their campaign but they still lost. Why? Well even now they would go to the mat denying it but there's only one explanation – we were offering something better.

If it wasn't for Thomas Mair I'm guessing we would have won by about 6% and because referenda tend to confirm the status quo, if Britain were an independent nation voting whether or not to *join* the EU, independence would win by around 65/35. Seriously. Remain were lucky they weren't thrashed, so they shouldn't wonder where their campaign went wrong because it didn't, their campaign was pretty effective, so much so that they managed to get 48% of voters to endorse a dysfunctional political construct that was destroying Europe for all the world to see.

Here are the Brighton Brexiteers. Ok, so regarding the six people in this photograph. Is that why we won? Well yes and no. The margin of victory was over a million votes so even if none of the Brighton team had done anything we still would have won, but the important point is that there were lots of other autonomous leaderless ramshackle outfits just like us up and down the country.

When the history of the Revolution is written, it will be tempting for someone like Max Hastings to simplify the story into a narrative where one individual (Farage or Johnson) led the peasants to a stunning victory. They didn't. The war was won not by one great leader but by thousands of nobodies who incrementally broke down a vast institutionalised lie. My essays had about 14,000 hits on my blog, if we add to that the hits from GBrexit that brings us up to about 150,000. Now let's add all the hits for other people's articles I shared, and all the leaflets I gave out, all the blogging and tweeting and the way people I persuaded then passed on the same information to others. Obviously, this is a rough science, but I got information to about 160,000 people. Now let's presume I had a 0.5% success rate. 800 votes? Seems realistic. Now let's presume 2000 other Brexiteers like Paul and Vicki were doing the same. 2000 x 800 = 1,600,000. There's your margin of victory.

Ok so why did I bother to include all the stuff about the leaking roof, and losing my computer file and the pregnancy? Because I want a big pat on the back for being so exceptional? No, the opposite in fact – it is actually lovely to go back to obscurity again, I never check Facebook or Twitter or my blog stats anymore. I get maybe a couple of emails a week, but no *'likes' 'hits'* or *'shares'*, no texts, no phone calls – it's heaven! I take my children to the park, watch them grow up, and support the wife who supported me. No, I didn't include all that stuff to garner praise – the whole point isn't that I made an exceptional contribution – but that I *didn't* make an exceptional contribution! There were loads of people like me in every town, each one of whom had *their* leaking roofs to fix and *their* kids to look after and *their* bills to pay and *their* shit to deal with, who just like me were demoralised and made loads of fuck ups, but who, out of sheer bloody-mindedness just plodded on, conversation by conversation, vote by vote until the tide was turned, and this story is as much theirs as mine.

The point I'm making is this: if reader, you are young then one day a revolution will present itself to you, so I'm just giving you the heads-up that it will not happen at a convenient time; you will be in the middle of things, you will have commitments, and you will have your hands full. But when that day comes you will have a choice: either do your best or wish you had done your best. Good luck, but don't believe the romantic view of revolutions, it's not about dressing like Che Guevara, significant things are assembled from mundane elements.

So, this is my last handy tip for all you would-be revolutionaries out there, and it's probably the most important tip of all: be right. You can survive being unfashionable, you can survive being unpopular, but being on the wrong side of history is fatal, so if all the cool people are advocating something, before you jump on board just ask yourself this question: *which path will mean the most people have the most scrutiny over the most power?* And you may not like the answer, you may not *want* the answer, but if you don't stand by it then get ready to follow Paul Mason and Owen Jones off the edge of the world where the ignominy of history awaits.

Finally, I have heard that some parents really have named their babies Brexit. If it is true then may their days be many and happy.

The people in the above photo are (from left to right) Paul, Peter, Ian, me, Vicki and Wayne (often out-numbered, never out-gunned).

10 DOWNING STREET
LONDON SW1A 2AA

THE PRIME MINISTER

5 March 2015

Dear Sebastian,

Congratulations!

I am delighted to be recognising you as the 237th UK Point of Light.

UK Points of Light is a national award which recognises outstanding individual volunteers - points of light in our country - who are doing extraordinary things in the service of others.

Your innovative overhaul of an iconic red K2 British phone box has created a fantastic resource for the whole community. Thanks to your efforts Lewisham is now home to London's smallest library, open 24 hours a day, 365 days a year!

I believe it is my duty as Prime Minister to hold up examples of great volunteering and service as an inspiration to others. Through your hard work and dedication you are making our communities stronger, and our country a better place.

On behalf of the whole country, I hope this Points of Light Award can be a small way of saying thank you.

With all good wishes,

Yours,

David

Sebastian Handley

160